Women & Power

JAN DARGATZ

OLIVER
NELSON

THOMAS NELSON PUBLISHERS
Nashville • Atlanta • London • Vancouver

To

Abigail, Amy, Catherine, Christi,
Gillian, Hannah, Johanna, Joy,
Katelyn, Kiersten, Kimmi,
Laurel, Mary, Rachel, and Sara.

*May you always be truly righteous
women who use your God-given power for
divine and eternal purposes.*

Published in Nashville, Tennessee, by Thomas Nelson, Inc., Publishers, and distributed in Canada by Word Communications, Ltd., Richmond, British Columbia.

The Bible version used in this publication is THE NEW KING JAMES VERSION. Copyright © 1979, 1980, 1982, 1990, Thomas Nelson, Inc., Publishers.

Library of Congress Cataloging-in-Publication Data

Dargatz, Jan Lynette.
    Women and power / Jan Dargatz.
       p. cm.
    ISBN 0-7852-8008-1 (pbk.)
    1. Women—Religious life. 2. Power—Religious aspects—Christianity.
I. Title.
BV4527.D35 1995
248.8'43—dc20
                                       95–2564
                                        CIP

Printed in the United States of America.
1 2 3 4 5 6 — 00 99 98 97 96 95

Contents

1

Women Have What It Takes

My mouth turned dry.
My palms got sweaty.
My heart pounded.
My vision blurred.
I panicked!

It happened more than thirty years ago, but I remember the experience as if it were yesterday. I was struck with stage fright for the first time in my life.

I was a finalist in a state-wide speech contest, and as luck would have it, I was scheduled to speak last. Such a position meant, of course, that I had to listen to all of the other speakers before I had my turn at the podium.

Now, I was no amateur at speaking or performing, and I was no stranger to competition. Crowds had never frightened me before.

In prior speech contests, however, position had always worked in my favor. I was generally in the middle of a competitive lineup, and I usually heard at least one speaker about whom I would conclude, *I can do better than that*. This time, however, all of the speakers who spoke before me were excellent. There wasn't a weak speaker in the group!

During the speech immediately preceding mine, I caught the eye of my father, who was seated in the back of the room. Dad had somehow stumbled into the role of my coach and mentor at these events. The high school speech teacher didn't have time to attend out-of-town competitions, although it was her idea that I enter them on behalf of the school. My mother found the experience of being an audience member nerve-racking and felt she would be more of a hindrance than a help at performance time, so she opted to stay at home with my younger brother. As a result, Dad and I had to "go it alone." That was fine with me. I loved going places with my father and I agreed with my mother's arguments. Besides, Dad always seemed to know instinctively how to inspire me to do my best, and he knew what made for a good speech. He almost always called the scoring and placement as the judges did, and many of the other speech coaches actually thought he was a fellow speech teacher. When he caught my eye that night, he knew I was in deep trouble.

During the three-minute interval allotted between speakers, he walked to the side of the platform and from offstage he whispered to me, "Jannie, you've got what it takes."

You've got what it takes. What did Dad mean exactly? *What did I have?* At that point, I could barely remember my name, much less my speech. *How did I get it?* I had never been in this predicament before. *Why me?* The thought had already crossed my mind that I had never really asked to compete in speechmaking, so what was I doing here anyway?

In retrospect, I believe that Dad didn't have a clue either as to any logical, rational meaning for that phrase on that particular night. Still, the phrase took root someplace deep within my being. I believed what my father told me, and his words gave me a courage I did not have just moments before. Although the phrase may not have had a great deal of intellectual meaning, it had worlds of emotional, psychological, and even spiritual meaning to me.

Speakers often report that they have butterflies in their stomachs. My stage fright panic felt more like a butter churn at work. But when I took Dad's words as truth, the butter churn inside me turned into a generator. A sense of determination and *inner power* took hold of me. I truly felt powerful as I faced that audience. And I gave a whale of a speech.

I don't recall what place I took in the competition that night. I have a difficult time connecting specific memories with the trophies that remain on the shelf above the closet of my childhood bedroom. But I do know this: I have never had stage fright since then. Any time I have sensed the onset of even the least bit of panic, Dad's words have come roaring back to my mind—*You've got what it takes.*

"To have what it takes" is my definition of power. A woman has power when she can get a job done, when she accomplishes a goal, when she can do what she desires to do to the best of her ability, and when she has an inner knowing that she is not only worthy but also capable of doing whatever the Lord asks her to do.

If you have never heard it before, let me assure you today:

···

Women have what it takes.

···

And more specifically, *you* have what it takes if you have Jesus Christ as your Savior and Lord.

Your power as a Christian woman is vastly more potent than your power as an ordinary woman. It is Christ's presence that makes your power extraordinary, truly effective, and awesome both to experience and to behold. Christ promises to work not only in you, but also through you, to accomplish His purposes on this earth.

You are His means of getting the job done. He has chosen

you for the task. He has equipped you to act. And He says to you today as His woman on this earth, "My beloved one, you have what it takes."

. . . .

Power Is Not Something You Need to *Get*— You Already Have It!

Very often in today's discussions about women and power, the focus is placed on what women *don't* have. The concerns are usually with a lack of political clout, corporate opportunity, privilege in the church, funding for medical research, or simple social respect. All of these are legitimate concerns, but to a great extent these issues lie "outside" a woman. They are rooted generally in a woman feeling that somebody else is hurting her or limiting her—and thus, somebody else is responsible for her weakness or lack of power.

Rather than focus on outer signs of power that women might think they don't have, this book focuses on the inner power that women *do* have. This type of power manifests itself in many ways, toward many ends. An incident in my childhood clearly demonstrated this tremendous inner power to me.

When I was in third grade, we had a bully in our class named Zelda. We don't often hear about female bullies, but Zelda was most definitely a bully. She was a big girl—actually, she had been held back a year so she was a year older and a year bigger than the rest of us. Even so, Zelda would have been big for a fourth grader! And she was mean-spirited.

Looking back, I have a great deal of sympathy for Zelda. She perhaps was the victim of an abusive home. No doubt she was lonely. She certainly hadn't been trained to express herself in positive ways that built friendships. In all likelihood, she was hurting emotionally and was desperate for our attention and love.

At the time, however, I thought and responded as all of the

other third graders. I thought Zelda was bad news, and definitely someone to be avoided.

Zelda especially seemed to enjoy picking on Janice, a small, frail girl who wore glasses and aced every spelling quiz. Janice was the female version of a nerd long before the word was coined.

It was a classic stereotypical matchup. Zelda would shove, and Janice would fall back, often falling all the way to the ground. Then Janice would pick herself up and run away while Zelda laughed . . . alone. Zelda had no friends, of course. We were all afraid of her, including the boys.

Zelda ruled the playground at recess, with a swagger and a laugh, but nary a word . . . until the day when Janice stood her ground.

Janice saw Zelda coming and she planted her feet, one foot a step in front of the other, and she leaned in toward Zelda so that when Zelda shoved, Janice didn't budge. Zelda didn't know what to do. She had never encountered resistance before, and she obviously hadn't thought about the possibility of using her fists and slugging Janice in the face. She shoved again, but Janice didn't go down. Zelda shoved a third time, and as any third grader should have known, a third shove was long enough for the teacher monitoring recess to see what was happening.

Zelda was marched to the principal's office and Janice was hailed as a hero.

Janice didn't have to fight for her rights. She simply had to resist. The issue was not truly one of the power Zelda exerted over Janice, but of the inner power that Janice developed in taking her stand against Zelda. Zelda was still bigger and stronger than Janice, but Janice was more powerful.

Now, Janice could have lobbied for a wall to be built between her and Zelda, or for the playground to be divided into Zelda territory and Janice territory. She could have rallied others to create a hate campaign against Zelda. She could have insisted that the teacher monitor her every move, or Zelda's every move.

In taking any of those approaches, Janice might have curtailed Zelda's power over her and she may have gained a little more playground freedom, but she would *not* have developed any inner fortitude—and certainly not a feeling of inner power that might transfer to other situations and other people. The power that Janice developed was a power that no doubt has remained with her and has been applied numerous times through the years. It was a power of character, of inner strength. It was lasting, genuine, right-is-on-my-side power.

Whenever I hear a woman tell me what women can't do, or begin to tell me about the "bullies" that keep women down, I think of Zelda and Janice. The gains that women may achieve by insisting that men bully them less or that an impartial higher authority level the playing field are gains that may give women more privileges, but not necessarily more genuine power. They are gains that are outside the individual woman and women as a whole.

True power is an inner quality, not something marked by rule, regulation, or protective relationship. It's the power akin to that of steel girders in a building—no visible manifestation, but tremendous strength to withstand storm or shaking earth.

It's the power of bone inside body—no protrusions, but stature, structure, and flexibility nonetheless.

It's the power of character, fortitude, resolve, determination, self-confidence, and courage.

It's the inner power that a woman knows to be true of herself, regardless of circumstances and situations.

True power causes a woman to think, "I have what it takes," regardless of what others may say. To one woman it may be having what it takes to resist, to endure, to persist, to survive. To another it may mean having what it takes to achieve, to train, and to win the victory. To one it might mean having the courage to last for the long haul, and to another, having the courage to let go and move on.

Ultimately, it is power that is defined within, without regard to any other person except the Lord Jesus Christ.

From this perspective of power, this book has one overriding message for all Christian women:

....

You have both the authority and ability to get things done.

....

Two key words in this statement warrant further definition. *Authority* refers to the fact that women have the right and privilege to act in certain arenas. These arenas differ according to the individual. This book assumes, however, that there is one arena in which all Christian women have authority to function to their maximum potential, and that is in the kingdom of God—God's domain in the world today.

Ability refers to the fact that women have skills, knowledge, and talent to act effectively. Women are creative. They are rational, logical, and brilliant intellectually. They are sensitive, intuitive, and loving. They are physically able, spiritually adept, emotionally capable, and psychologically qualified. Individually, each woman is a one-of-a-kind combination of an infinite number of unique traits—from the genetic code of each cell, to the particular moment of her birth, to her destined role within God's eternity.

To fully understand the definition of these terms, it is important to know the Source of a woman's authority and ability.

....

The Source of a Woman's Authority

For Christian women, the question of authority is an especially important one because, like Christian men, we do not rely on our *selves* as the source of our own authority. Neither did Jesus, the role model we share with men. Our authority flows from God the Father. Because we live on the resurrection side of the Cross, our authority flows from the Father through our belief in His Son, Jesus Christ, who tells us plainly in His Word that He has empowered His people with the Holy Spirit. As Christian women, we act on behalf of Christ. We are His witnesses, His people, His daughters, His beloved disciples. We are His presence in this world. In fact, the Lord calls us to be His very body alive and functioning on the earth today.

We are to go and do and say only as the Spirit directs us. Our lives are no longer our own. We do His will. And thus, the arenas in which we exercise authority are defined by Him, not us. Those arenas may change from time to time. They do so at His discretion. Our influence may be greater or lesser in certain situations or relationships. Our influence fluctuates according to His gauge.

The broad-stroked, general attributes of that relationship and our authority in Christ Jesus are clearly detailed and illustrated in God's Word. It is to God's Word that we turn for examples of how we as women can best express God's power in and through our lives.

One thing we quickly discover in studying God's Word is that at no time do we find limitations placed upon women who are operating *in the Spirit*. The prophet Joel foresaw the day in which we live:

> "And it shall come to pass afterward
> That I will pour out My Spirit on all flesh;
> . . . on My menservants and on My maidservants
> I will pour out My Spirit in those days."
> (Joel 2:28–29)

The Holy Spirit is the One who presents needs to us, and He then pours His gifts through us to meet those needs. As Acts 1:8 tells us, we each receive power "when the Holy Spirit has come upon [us]," and the purpose of that power is to make us Christ's witnesses.

We can and must ask the Holy Spirit in each circumstance or situation we face, "What is my authority as a Christian woman in this situation?" In one situation, He may direct us to make a decision. In another, He may direct us to acquiesce to the directive of another person. In one relationship, He may direct us to lead. In another, He may direct us to follow. In one circumstance, He may have us speak boldly. In another, He may have us remain silent.

Jesus gave no blanket rules that are gender based. Paul's teachings, which may appear to be gender biased to twentieth-century readers, were often rooted in his desire to blend Gentile and Jewish believers into one Church, or to illustrate the Lordship of Jesus Christ over His Church. Read the Word closely and in full context. Women remain "free to be subject" to God's Spirit in all things and at all times. It is to Him that we must listen, and listen closely. And it is to the Holy Spirit of Almighty God that we owe our ultimate allegiance and obedience.

....

The Source of a Woman's Ability

Not only does the Spirit give women authority, but He also gives women the ability to exercise that authority. The Holy Spirit is the ultimate Courage Builder, Gift Giver, Fortitude Founder, and Strength Endower. The omnipotent infinite Spirit bestows God's power on us, in finite form to fit our finite frame, so that we might bear His authority into our finite world.

As Christian women, we must always look to God as the Source of our ability. He is our Creator, the One who made each of us unique in talent, ability, and circumstance. He is the Divine Orchestrator, who not only has given us the ability to play well the instrument that is our life, but who also has grouped us so that we might play His song to touch the human heart and woo the world to Him.

Functionally, women and men were designed to *complement* each other and to *complete* each other in their abilities. Before God, and with regard to all of the rights and privileges pertaining to forgiveness by God and reconciliation to God, to the redemption and transformation of the soul, to the manifestation of the gifts and the bearing of the fruit of the Holy Spirit, and to the promise of eternal life, women stand equal to men. In functional matters pertaining to church organization and family roles, theological interpretations differ. These differences relate, however, to what a woman *does* with her abilities, not to whether she does or does not have abilities.

Lines of authority in Scripture are drawn on the basis of decision-making protocol, not on the basis of ability. Having different abilities and using abilities differently are two distinct things!

Consider a group of five women. Each of them has an ability to contribute toward preparing a meal. One will be better at organizing the menu, another at baking the bread, another at preparing dessert, and so forth. But one person will need to have authority to make decisions and parcel out assignments according to abilities. So it is with a family and a church. Ability is not the issue—rather, it is diversity of roles in accomplishing tasks.

If we compare talents from person to person, we will find diversity. Rarely, however, should we generalize those differences to say that all women or all men are better in one area of ability. The issue is usually not who is more able because of sex. The issue is nearly always one of who is more able in the moment and at the particular task.

Three Important Questions to Ask About Your Ability

When you think about an ability, there are three important questions to consider:

- Can *I* do this?
- Can *all* women do this?
- Can *any* woman do this?

You can do some things in ways and to degrees nobody else can. You will have some opportunities and face some decisions that no other person will.

Are there some things that all women can do? Yes. This book describes eight types of power that all women have. When it comes to doing specific tasks, however, not all women can do all things. Not all women can cook well, sew well, or clean house well. (Not all men can, either.)

You may find that your answer to the first two questions is sometimes yes, sometimes no, but the answer to the third question is nearly always yes. Apart from certain biological functions, a woman somewhere on the planet earth can probably do just about anything. Some women are gifted in extraordinary ways.

Can a woman lead a department in a corporation or a university? Of course.

Can a woman found a company and be its CEO? Of course.

Can a woman be a judge, lead an army, or lead a nation? Of course.

Can a woman give a spiritually authoritative word from God to other people? Of course—that's what the gifts of prophecy, word of knowledge, and word of wisdom are all about.

Can a woman make decisions regarding the fate and future of her own life, as well as the lives of her children and family? Of course.

And in some cases a woman can do these things better than all other women of her time, and better than the men, too.

On what basis do I make these claims? On the basis that examples of each of these roles for a woman are given in God's Word. At other times, and in very specific functional roles, God's Word advises women that they are *not* to fulfill a certain role or take on a certain responsibility. In virtually all cases, this is not a limitation for womankind nearly as much as it is a protection or privilege for women in that context or function.

The ways in which women are to use abilities also differ functionally, practically, and organizationally. These differences are nearly always time and context specific, with great variations existing from person to person and group to group.

The point, of course, is to know when to use your abilities, and *how*. Not all abilities are to be used at all times, but all abilities are to be used at all *appropriate* times!

The bottom line is that women have abilities and they are to use the abilities they have. The goal is for each woman to *maximize* her abilities and to use them to the utmost wherever and whenever she can.

If a woman keeps her focus on maximizing her abilities and then uses them to impact her world, she most likely will find that she has very little time or energy left over to be concerned about what others say she *cannot* be or do. She will become so busy and so focused on *doing* that she actually has very little awareness of others who may be intent on thwarting her or insulting her along the way. She is strong from the inside out—as opposed to being made strong from the outside in. Like Janice, she becomes more intent on standing up to the Zeldas of this world than she is concerned about the consequences of falling or failing.

....

Types of Power Women Have

In my opinion, women have at least eight types of power. Again, any individual woman bears these types of power in varying degrees. Still, I have yet to meet a woman who did not have at least a degree of each of these eight types of power.

1. The power to influence
2. The power to seduce

3. The power to subdue
4. The power to transact
5. The power to train
6. The power to witness
7. The power to pray
8. The power to persevere

Now, there may be other types of power common to all women. I make no claim that these are the only powers that all women have. About these eight, however, I have a great deal of confidence. Why? First, because I readily can find examples of these powers at work in women of the Bible. Second, I have yet to meet a woman who took an honest, self-exploratory look into the mirror of her own soul and then said, speaking intuitively and honestly about herself, "I don't have that ability at all."

God's Word says by example and illustration that these types of power have been given to women without regard to culture, age, race, or nationality. Furthermore, women universally know at the core of their beings that they have these types of power. This book simply serves to remind Christian women of who they already are and what they already possess.

Please note, too, that I am not claiming that women alone have these powers. Men may very well possess some or all of them, too. My goal, however, is not to compare men and women, but to explore the inner power made available by God to all women.

Finally, when I make the assumption that women already possess power—these areas of authority and these types of abilities—I am also making this very basic claim about power: Women do not need to go out and get power. Rather, they need to recognize they have power in these areas, and then strengthen their power and use it.

We hear a great deal today about empowerment and how

women need to demand, or otherwise acquire, some power and then more power and then still more power.

A woman has all the raw latent power she will ever need to accomplish all that the Lord has asked her to do. She has already been endowed with this power by her Creator. Her challenge is to grow, refine, and focus her ability to apply this power.

Consider your intelligence—your ability to learn, understand, and reason. It would sound silly to you if I said, "Go out and get some intelligence." You already have intelligence. You were born with it.

What you have to do is *use* your intelligence—develop it through education and experience, and apply it to solving problems and meeting needs.

The same goes for faith. The Scriptures tell us that each person is given a "measure" of faith. We are born with the ability to believe in things, for things, and about things. For me to say "Go get faith" would be to advise you to go out and get something you already have!

That isn't what the Lord compels us to do. Rather, He asks us to grow in faith, even to develop great faith, and to become people who use our faith to bring deliverance and health—in the broadest and most inclusive definitions of those words—to ourselves and to others.

In like manner, you have creativity. You may not recognize that fact, but you have it nonetheless. Consider that every time you make a statement, you string together words in a creative way. You make a statement that is unique in the time and context of both your personal history and the history of the world! This is true even if you are reciting a well-known hymn, Bible verse, prayer, or the pledge of allegiance. Each statement you make is a creative act, the result of your volition of will, uttered in a unique context and moment in time.

Everything about your expression to the world is unique each and every day of your life. That's being creative! You were born with that ability. How you choose to exercise it, develop it, and use your creativity to impact others is up to you.

And so it is with power. You were born with it. You just need to recognize it, and then use your power wisely.

Each of the eight powers is neutral in and of itself. Each can be used in a good way or a bad way. For example, the power to persevere can be used for good if it means enduring to the end for a godly purpose. It can also be sheer stubbornness, or a refusal to be budged into doing God's will!

As another example, the power to transact can be used negatively—for selfish or evil ends. Or it can be used to win souls and meet needs.

The underlying motivation for using power—and the end to which it is aimed—is not something that a woman faces once in her life. It is an issue that arises again and again, sometimes on a daily basis. My will or Thine? Right or wrong? For self or others? We are all pulled in one direction or another on a nearly constant basis.

In other words, a woman cannot make a one-time vow, "I'll use all my power for God's purposes," as some kind of immunity shot against future temptation or neglect.

The phrase, "power corrupts," isn't true from God's perspective! God, the Source of all power, is absolute and never corrupt. He calls us to use power and not be corrupted by it. We must come again and again to the decision, "I will use power for good, not evil. I choose not to be corrupted by power." The choice is ours to make, but we must make it intentionally and seriously if our exercise of power is to be for righteous ends.

....
What Are Women to Do with Their Power?

Once a woman recognizes and accepts the fact that she has God-given power—again, both the authority to take action and the ability to act—she has to ask herself three questions:

- Will I develop my God-given power?
- Will I grow in my abilities and seek to apply them in as many ways as possible in areas where I am authorized by God to take action?
- Will I exercise my power?

Frankly, some women choose to be weak, even when confronted with the fact that they aren't weak and were never created to be weak. Weakness works for some women. They use it to manipulate others.

Manipulation Isn't True Power

Manipulation is an aberrant, ungodly use of power. This doesn't mean that manipulation isn't effective or doesn't work. It can be and does! A woman might use manipulation as a technique to get what she wants, but manipulation is neither rooted in healthy self-esteem nor is it a technique sanctioned by God's Word. Even though it might accomplish a short-term goal, manipulation, in the long run, injures both the person being manipulated and the one doing the manipulating. How so? Because manipulation isn't honest. The person may say, "If you don't do this, I will do that." In such cases, the person making such a statement is usually making an idle threat. Idle threats are ultimately lies.

Or, the person may say, "I need you to do this, because I can't do it for myself." In fact, the person usually *can* take action, even if it is limited action. She simply doesn't want to do so. If a person has a genuine need, however, the request isn't manipulation. It's a plea, which *is* a legitimate aspect of the power to conduct transactions.

To fully embrace the potential of one's power means that a woman must be willing to take risks related to her power and be willing to grow and change. Not all women are willing to do that. Just knowing that she has power does not make her more powerful. She must choose to develop and use her power, and in using power wisely, she grows in power. The same is true for faith, creativity, and intelligence. The more a woman exercises and trains these potentialities, the more she grows and changes as a person, and the more powerful her faith, creative ability, and mental ability become.

If a woman chooses to use her God-given power she faces a decision regarding *how* she will use her power. In other words, she must answer the question, "Will I use my power in ways that correspond with God's Word, or will I use my power without regard to the Lord's purposes and plans?"

In theory, most Christian women will say, "Of course I'll use my power for God's purposes." In practice, however, we often find ourselves with a desire to go our own way and fulfill our own wishes. We all face the struggle of choosing to do that which we know is pleasing to the Lord, rather than choosing to do what pleases our own appetites, lusts, greed, pride, and desire for fame and glory.

If a woman recognizes her power and ardently seeks to use it in ways that are pleasing to the Lord, she faces a decision as to *what* she should do, and *when* in obedience to the Lord's directives in her life. This decision is often a daily one.

Here is where the rubber meets the road, so to speak. Knowing we have power and wanting to please the Lord take us to the point where we actually must discern and then decide *how* we are going to exert our power to build the kingdom of God. What will we do with the power we have? How will we manifest it?

Some women I know channel their God-given power into organizations. They perform tasks that propel institutions and people forward in their lives. Others channel their power into presentations, performances, or conference speaking. Still others channel their power into written words. Some paint or illustrate. Still others make intercessory prayer their means of exerting power in the world. And many women do a combination of things—answering requests, responding to the needs of others, and giving in whatever ways possible, using whatever means are available.

In most cases, the truly powerful Christian woman will manifest her power in ways that do not call attention to the acts of power or to the woman herself. Instead, the way she uses power will call attention to Christ Jesus. The glory, the kingdom, and the power will ultimately be aimed toward, given to, and then viewed as flowing from the Lord God Almighty!

This in no way implies that the woman has conned the world. Rather, it means she has chosen totally to subsume her power under the broader umbrella of the Lord's power. She exerts her power in a way that gets His job accomplished, as opposed to accomplishing her own agenda in life.

For this to happen, a woman needs first to know what it is that the Lord has asked her to do. She also must discern when, with whom, and how she is to take action. And then, she must do what she does with the greatest amount of efficiency and effectiveness, all cloaked in a gorgeous garment of graciousness.

Power Cloaked by Graciousness

Graciousness is that wonderful quality that tempers and beautifies the raw energy of power. It doesn't diminish power. Rather, it makes power palatable and acceptable to others.

Graciousness is the sleek chassis and luxurious interior that accompanies the 450 horsepower engine. (A woman's choice in automobiles, the advertisers and marketers now tell us, reflects a woman's concept of her own womanhood.)

Graciousness is like a high-energy meal that is presented and served in a way that is polished, polite, and appealing. Graciousness is like the digestible coating on the high-potency vitamin tablet.

Graciousness is evidenced in the beauty that adorns centers of decision making and problem solving.

Graciousness is the manner in which criticisms are spoken so as not to offend, but rather, to encourage and compel.

Graciousness is the way in which disputes are resolved so that relationships remain firmly rooted in love, yet grow toward perfection.

Graciousness is speaking the truth in such a way that it might be heard and pondered.

A truly powerful Christian woman is both gracious and generous. She displays an overflowing, always-giving-to-others, fountainlike abundance of all of the fruit of the Holy Spirit in her life: love, joy, peace, long-suffering, kindness, goodness, faithfulness, gentleness, and self-control. (See Gal. 5:22–23.) But, she does so with a resolve about purity, holiness, and righteousness that cannot be shaken.

She does not compromise God's Word. She keeps God's commandments and teaches them to others. She focuses her efforts toward accomplishing the Lord's ends. She proclaims what is right, even if it means putting her own reputation on the line. She says no to sin, rather than attempting to justify it. She repents when she errs and forgives freely. In sum, the truly powerful Christian woman must first be a *true Christian*. She must be a woman in pursuit of righteousness, not power . . . a woman who longs to manifest Christ's love to the world, not her own grandeur.

Power grows in a woman as the result of right believing and right actions. And right believing and right actions temper expressions of power.

The most powerful Christian women I know are women who actually do and say very little, but their very presence is commanding and their love is compelling.

The quote made famous by Theodore Roosevelt states, "Speak softly and carry a big stick; you will go far." That's not what Christ asks of us, however.

The genuinely powerful Christian woman speaks both boldly and softly, carries no stick, and has a resolve about her faith that cannot be shaken and a will of iron toward accomplishing what she perceives to be her God-given destiny.

In this manner, her strength becomes appealing. And in the end, she "has what it takes." She gets the job done. She wins the argument, takes the position, gains the favor, earns the approval, and takes enemy territory for the Lord.

The ground she gains may be only a small parcel of enemy territory. It may be an entire region "in the heavenlies." Regardless of the size of the victory, her victory is the Lord's victory. And her reward is an even greater awareness of His presence and His purpose for her life.

The truly powerful Christian woman always moves forward in her life and in her efforts to expand the kingdom of God.

Are you aware today of the power God has given you? Do you desire to grow in it? Do you long to use it for the Lord's purposes? If so . . . read on! And remember with each turn of the page . . . you *have* this power as your heritage in Christ Jesus. You can grow in this power, and you can *use* it for His kingdom's sake.

2

·················

The
Power to
Influence

Much is said today about *control*. Women want to control their own destinies, their own bodies, and certain political processes or organizations. The right of determination—the right to make the final choice and call the shots—is regarded as the ultimate in the power of decision making. The word *influence* seems to pale in comparison to the words *control* and *determination*. What we need to recognize anew is that the person who influences the most is indeed the one who controls and determines!

Influence is the power behind the throne. It's the reason behind the action. Influence is sometimes veiled power, but it is power nonetheless. And as with all types of power, influence can be rooted in good or evil intentions, and aimed at good or evil outcomes. The Bible provides numerous examples of women who exhibited influence for good and for evil.

·················

Two Influencers of Evil: Jezebel and Athaliah

One of the most notable influencers toward evil was Jezebel. In fact, Jezebel's very name has become synonymous with evil influence.

The core of Jezebel's influence was spiritual. The Scriptures tell us that Ahab took Jezebel as his wife. What really happened was that Ahab took Jezebel as his spiritual director, and Jezebel worshiped Baal. Ahab built an altar to Baal, a temple to Baal, and set up a wooden image of Baal for purposes of worship. A temple, altar, and image of Baal, of course, mean nothing unless the people are led, through either decree or example, to worship Baal. Jezebel and Ahab certainly provided that leadership. Worship of Baal necessitated a vast number of priests to conduct the necessary rituals. Baal worship was not a private activity for Jezebel and Ahab. Baal worship became the religion of the land and the foremost ceremonial function for this king and queen.

The writers of the Bible conclude that through these actions, "Ahab did more to provoke the LORD God of Israel to anger than all the kings of Israel who were before him" (1 Kings 16:33).

When Elijah confronted 450 prophets of Baal and killed them in a great spiritual victory atop Mount Carmel, Jezebel obviously was not amused. She made a solemn oath to kill Elijah, and Elijah fled for his life.

Jezebel's evil influence did not end until after her husband and her son were both killed. She died a hideous death, thrown from a window in her palace, trampled by a horse, and eaten by dogs to the point where only her skull, feet, and the palms of her hands remained to be buried.

Jezebel's influence did not lead to the destruction of Israel, but it did lead to the end of the royal line for her husband's family and her own heirs. Elisha's prophetic words from the Lord came to pass: "For the whole house of Ahab shall perish; and I will cut off from Ahab all the males in Israel, both bond and free" (2 Kings 9:8). Jehu was anointed king, and he pierced the heart of Joram, Jezebel's son, with an arrow. It was Jehu's horse that trampled Jezebel in the street. Jehu also destroyed the seventy "sons" of Ahab, as well as all his great men and close acquaintances and his priests. (See 2 Kings 10:7,11.)

Jezebel's evil influence destroyed her family.

Another woman in the Scriptures who exerted her influence for evil purposes was Athaliah. Athaliah was the mother of Ahaziah, who had come to the throne of Judah after his father died of an incurable disease. Ahaziah was only twenty-two years old when he assumed the throne, and apparently his mother had enormous influence over him. In 2 Chronicles 22:3 we read that Ahaziah "walked in the ways of the house of Ahab, for his mother advised him to do wickedly."

Walked in the ways of the house of *Ahab?* How could this be? Ahaziah was in Judah. Ahab ruled over Israel.

Well. . . . Athaliah was the daughter of Ahab and Jezebel. Like mother, like daughter. Athaliah had married for political purposes and had great political ambition. When her son Ahaziah was killed by Joram, Athaliah immediately took control. The Scriptures tell us that "she arose and destroyed all the royal heirs" (2 Kings 11:1). In other words, she had everyone in her family killed, including her own grandchildren. She wanted no opposition to the throne of Israel, and she ruled with an evil and iron hand for six years. She is the only woman ever to sit on David's throne, and her reign was marked by evil from start to finish. She even had a portion of the Temple pulled down to build a structure for Baal worship.

Unknown to Athaliah, one of her grandsons had escaped the massacre of the royal family. When this child, Joash, was seven years old, the high priests in Jerusalem proclaimed him to be king. A great celebration was held in the Temple of God, and when Athaliah heard news of the coronation, she rushed in the Temple shouting, "Treason!" It's difficult to imagine a more ungrandmotherly scene. Athaliah's shout was intended to be a death sentence for young Joash. Instead, the priests decreed that Athaliah be killed, but not in the house of God. As she ran from the Temple, she was killed at the horses' gate.

Both Jezebel and Athaliah destroyed their families: one primarily through her evil spiritual influence and the other through her great desire for political dominance.

Esther stands in stark contrast to these women.

. . . .

Esther's Great Influence for Good

A recent survey in the United States compared the achievement levels of boys with that of girls and found that boys and girls are equal in achievement in virtually all areas of study until they reach their teenage years. Then, boys begin to outperform girls in test scores and grades. Those conducting the study concluded that the difference occurs because boys are encouraged to take risks and girls are not.

Esther was a woman who was encouraged to take a risk and courageous enough to take it.

As the young and beautiful queen of King Ahasuerus, Esther had access to power, but no direct power herself. Word came to her that her cousin Mordecai, who had raised and protected Esther after the death of her parents, had put on sackcloth and ashes and was crying with a loud and bitter voice throughout the city. Esther immediately sent garments to clothe Mordecai, but he would not accept them. Then Esther called one of the king's eunuchs, Hathach, who had been appointed to attend her, and dispatched him to find out what was happening. Mordecai told Hathach of Haman's plot to destroy all the Jews in the land. Haman, as the chief of all King Ahasuerus's princes, had been given the king's signet ring to authorize the slaughter.

Mordecai gave Hathach a written copy of the decree authorizing the destruction of the Jews, and he requested that Hathach command Esther to make a supplication to the king and plead for him and for her people. Hathach returned and told Esther all that Mordecai had said and she sent back this message to Mordecai:

"All the king's servants and the people of the king's provinces know that any man or woman who goes into the inner court to the king, who has not been called, he has but one law: put all to death, except the one to whom the king holds out the golden scepter, that he may live. Yet I myself have not been called to go in to the king these thirty days." (Esther 4:11)

Esther no doubt felt that Mordecai didn't fully understand her situation in the court. Mordecai responded, however, by challenging Esther with life-or-death questions:

"Do not think in your heart that you will escape in the king's palace any more than all the other Jews. For if you remain completely silent at this time, relief and deliverance will arise for the Jews from another place, but you and your father's house will perish. Yet who knows whether you have come to the kingdom for such a time as this?" (Esther 4:13–14)

Mordecai laid the situation clearly before Esther: If you don't speak, you will surely perish. If you do speak up, who knows? Perhaps this is your destiny.

Esther had thought Mordecai didn't understand. Now she realized that she was the one who hadn't understood! A wise woman always faces up to and acknowledges her errors when they are brought to her attention.

Esther replied, "Go, gather all the Jews who are present in Shushan, and fast for me; neither eat nor drink for three days, night or day. My maids and I will fast likewise. And so I will go to the king, which is against the law; and if I perish, I perish!" (Esther 4:16).

Esther was willing to take the risk, but not without full spiritual preparation. Just as she had prepared herself physically for the possibility of being queen, she now prepared herself spiritually before facing the possibility of her death.

Esther fasted and prayed for three days, along with her many "prayer partners." We don't know if this is when the Lord gave her the fullness of the plan that eventually unfolded, but we do know that during her fasting time the Lord apparently revealed to her that she was to host a feast. We also can conclude that Esther relied solely on the Lord for direction and courage. No mention of advice from Mordecai or Hathach is given from this point forward in the story.

At the end of the three days, Esther put on her royal robes. These robes were not only beautiful to behold, but they also were indicative of her position as queen. Esther went to her unscheduled meeting with the king in the fullness of her own beauty and position.

When the king saw her standing in the court, he held out the golden scepter to her, and Esther moved closer and touched the top of the scepter. She was poised. She followed protocol.

The king asked her what she wanted. He would give her up to half of his kingdom. The king was in a generous mood, but Esther didn't ask for all that she wanted in that moment. Rather, she said, "If it pleases the king, let the king and Haman come today to the banquet that I have prepared for him" (Esther 5:4).

Esther was calling her man to dinner. The meal had been prepared and was ready for him. The king responded, "Bring Haman quickly, that he may do as Esther has said."

At dinner, King Ahasuerus asked Esther once again what he could do for her, and she responded by telling the king that she would prepare another banquet tomorrow and requested the attendance of the king and Haman.

Esther ordered a banquet while Haman ordered that gallows be built for Mordecai. That night, even as the gallows were being constructed, the king could not sleep. He asked that the book of records be brought to him and read to him. When he heard that Mordecai was the one who had told two of the king's eunuchs about an earlier plot to kill the king, he asked what had been done for Mordecai. The king's servants replied, "Nothing."

The king asked, "Who is in the court?" Haman had just

entered the court at that moment to recommend that Mordecai be hanged on the gallows he had prepared for him, so the servants replied, "Haman is there, standing in the court." The king told them to let Haman in. The king asked Haman what should be done to honor a man in whom the king delights. Haman assumed the king was talking about him, so he recommended that a royal robe be put on the man and that he be paraded through the city on a horse that the king had ridden. The king revealed that it was Mordecai he wished to honor in this manner, and Haman was forced to lead Mordecai through the city proclaiming as they went, "Thus shall it be done to the man whom the king delights to honor!"

Haman went home dejected, in utter humiliation. When he told his wife Zeresh and his friends what had happened, his wife gave him some good advice! She said, "If Mordecai, before whom you have begun to fall, is of Jewish descent, you will not prevail against him but will surely fall before him" (Esther 6:13*b*). How right she was! But Haman had no time to respond. He was late for dinner with Esther and the king.

During the second banquet, the king asked Esther for the third time, "What is your petition?" Again, he offered her up to half his kingdom.

Queen Esther answered him: "If I have found favor in your sight, O king, and if it pleases the king, let my life be given me at my petition, and my people at my request. For we have been sold, my people and I, to be destroyed, to be killed, and to be annihilated. Had we been sold as male and female slaves, I would have held my tongue, although the enemy could never compensate for the king's loss" (Esther 7:3–4).

The king asked Esther who would dare to do such a thing. Esther replied, "The adversary and enemy is this wicked Haman!"

Haman was terrified. His expression of fear may even have assured King Ahasuerus of his guilt. The king left the banquet room in a rage and went out into the garden. Haman was left standing before the queen, pleading for his life. In his impassioned plea, he fell across the couch where she was reclining, just as the king reentered the room. The king roared in fury, "Will he also assault the queen while I am in the house?"

The servants knew that Haman's fate was sealed, and they covered Haman's face as they prepared to escort him from the room. Harbonah, one of the eunuchs, said, "Look! The gallows, fifty cubits high, which Haman made for Mordecai . . . is standing at the house of Haman." The king ordered them to hang Haman on the gallows. So they hanged Haman and the king gave the "house of Haman" to Queen Esther.

Esther had an opportunity to tell the king that Mordecai was related to her, and Mordecai was brought before the king and queen. The king gave his signet ring—the same one he had given to Haman—to Mordecai, thus raising him to the highest appointed position in the land. Esther appointed Mordecai over the house of Haman.

Esther fell at the king's feet, and with tears she implored him to reverse the evil plot that Haman had devised against the Jews. The king held out the golden scepter to her, and she rose and stood before the king, making her petition again not as a wife, but as a queen. She said, "If it pleases the king, and if I have found favor in his sight and the thing seems right to the king and I am pleasing in his eyes, let it be written to revoke the letters devised by Haman, the son of Hammedatha the Agagite, which he wrote to annihilate the Jews who are in all the king's provinces. For how can I endure to see the evil that will come to my people? Or how can I endure to see the destruction of my countrymen?" (Esther 8:5–6).

The king responded to Esther and Mordecai, "Indeed, I have given Esther the house of Haman, and they have hanged him on the gallows because he tried to lay his hand on the Jews. You yourselves write a decree concerning the Jews, as you please, in the king's name, and seal it with the king's signet ring; for whatever is written in the king's name and sealed with the king's signet ring no one can revoke" (Esther 8:7–8).

The scribes were called, and the letter was written and sealed with the king's signet ring. It was distributed by couriers on royal horses, and the lives of the Jewish people were spared.

In less than a week, the fate of thousands of Jews had been changed and the chief enemy of the Jews had been defeated. Mordecai, a Jew, had risen to the number two position in the land. Queen Esther was exalted by her people and honored by her king and husband. In the days that followed, the king again asked Esther what more should be done for her and her people. She asked that Haman's ten sons be hanged on gallows as a sign to all the people that the Jews were not to be touched. And so it was done. Finally, Esther "wrote with full authority" the document that established Purim as a feast day among the Jewish people.

....

Maximizing Your Influence

The story of Esther illustrates several key points about how a woman can exercise influence.

Prepare in Advance

To exercise your influence effectively, you have to be intentional and plan in advance. It is not a matter of speaking off the top of your head. Esther took three days and nights to talk over with the Lord precisely what it was that He would have her do and say. She also made preparations for the banquet in advance.

Esther prepared herself spiritually and practically. You should do the same. Do your homework. Get your ducks in a row. Be prepared. Your influence will be greater.

A friend of mine in the corporate world was notoriously

known for her briefcase. People began to ask each other prior to meetings, "Did Carrie bring her briefcase?"

Carrie never went to a meeting unless she had researched a topic thoroughly and had prepared various computer printouts to support her opinions. Should a person give facts contrary to her research, she would calmly and graciously say, "Perhaps you can help me, then, with some discrepancies I have in my data bank." With that, she would pop open her briefcase atop the conference table, and pull out documents that were rarely refuted.

At other times, a person might ask her fairly belligerently, "On what do you base that opinion?" Up would come Carrie's briefcase, and out of it would come a supporting document.

Eventually the people with whom she worked began their meetings by asking her, "What do you have in your briefcase about this, Carrie?" This woman's influence was considerable, primarily because she had done her homework and others had not.

Be Confident and Act Professional

Esther didn't go to Ahasuerus as a wife to her husband. She went as a queen to her king. She didn't seek to gain her request through pillow talk. She went to his place of business.

You are wise to follow her example. Exercise influence with the utmost of professionalism. Dress as you would for the most important interview of your life. Go in the full confidence of your position. Take with you any documents you need, including any documents that verify your role, your concern, your position, your title, your official designation.

Esther followed the full protocol of the court. You are wise when you follow protocol, too.

Give Before You Make Requests

Esther found a way to please her king before she accepted his offer of a petition. She buttered the bread before handing him a slice.

What can you do for the person who is going to decide on the issue that is important to you? What can you give that is appropriate and within your authority to give? Make that gift!

Speak Personally

Esther didn't claim to be speaking on behalf of her people. She asked the king to spare her life, and for her sake—because it was her heartfelt plea—to spare her people.

Your personal story and personal feelings and concerns are the greatest strength you have in making a petition to a decision maker. Ask the person to do something that makes a difference in your life, and for others who are in your same situation.

Esther made no accusations. She didn't point her finger. She didn't ask for anything or anyone to be destroyed at first. She asked the king to make a decision for what was good and right.

To ask a person to spare life or to help someone is a far different petition than to ask a person to destroy life or crush someone. Esther gave the king a good choice to make. She asked for something that was easy for the king to give.

Be Direct and to the Point

Esther doesn't go into details or rehearse history. When the king asked who was attempting to destroy her and the Jews, she named Haman. In taking this simple, direct approach, Esther left the door open for King Ahasuerus to determine if Esther's charge was correct. Esther made no attempt to convince the king, or to pad the evidence against Haman. She simply named him.

Follow Esther's example. When you want to exercise your influence, be direct and to the point. The more streamlined the statement, the stronger it is.

Furthermore, Esther didn't ask that Haman be killed. She asked only that justice be done on her behalf, not that justice be done on his behalf. She gave the king the prerogative of sentencing and carrying out justice.

We are wise, too, when we let the decision maker determine just how, when, and by whom justice is to be exacted on our behalf.

This point probably cannot be overemphasized. It's vital when we seek to exert influence that we not force the hand of the decision maker, threaten him or her, or demand that our will be done.

Mary, the mother of Jesus, gives us a positive example of the balance between expressing a desire and leaving the decision up to the final decision maker. Mary and her family attended a wedding in Cana, very likely the wedding of a close relative. When the wine ran out, Mary sought out Jesus to report the situation. Jesus responded, "Woman, what does your concern have to do with Me? My hour has not yet come" (John 2:4). Mary didn't press her point with Jesus. She expressed what she had to say. Jesus was aware of the situation. She spoke instead to the servants, "Whatever He says to you, do it." Apparently she left the scene at that point.

Jesus responded to His mother's influence, telling the servants to fill the purification water jars with water, and then requesting that they draw out some of the contents of the jars and take it to the master of the feast. The water had become wine. (See John 2:1–10.)

Miriam, sister of Moses, also left the final decision freely in the hands of another. When her baby brother was plucked from the river by the maiden of Pharaoh's daughter, Miriam asked the right question, "Shall I go and call a nurse for you from the Hebrew women, that she may nurse the child for you?" (Exod. 2:7).

Miriam didn't offer a specific nurse, claim to know the baby, offer an explanation as to why he was floating in the river, cry, complain, protest, or take any action other than the most effective one. Pharaoh's daughter said, "Go." Miriam ran to her own mother. And when Jochebed showed up, Pharaoh's daughter said, "Take this child away and nurse him for me, and I will give you your wages" (Exod. 2:9).

In each case, these women made wise decisions about influence and the results were far reaching. Esther's people lived. Moses' life was saved, and he grew into the leader who took his people from slavery to a land of God's promise. Jesus' ministry of miracles began in Cana, giving Him a great platform on which to preach the good news of God's love for mankind.

Follow Through

Esther wasn't content to have Haman removed from power. She wanted the death sentence for her people removed. She followed through and got the decree she wanted, and later, she got the justice she wanted, and finally, she got the celebration she wanted . . . not only for herself, but for all her people.

Like Esther, you should not settle for less than what you know is right and good for you or others. As an influencer you must follow through and persevere.

....

Lessons About Influence from Other Bible Women

Three other Bible women teach us important aspects about the power of influence. Two of them teach us things *not* to do. One of them teaches us very positive things to do as we attempt to exert influence.

Job's Wife

Job's wife was a woman who attempted to exert influence. When her husband lost his seven sons and three daughters, all of his possessions, and then his own health, she said to her husband, "Do you still hold fast to your integrity? Curse God and die!" Her intent was to influence her husband to give up his beliefs about God and take his life and fate fully into his own hands.

Job responded, "You speak as one of the foolish women speaks. Shall we indeed accept good from God, and shall we not accept adversity?" (Job 2:10). Job refused to accept her influence . . . wisely so.

We are on very dangerous ground when we attempt to influence people to turn their backs on God and do their own thing with their lives. While we may not intend to discourage a person in his or her faith, we sometimes do so and may influence him or her toward evil in these ways:

- When we say to a person, "Oh, that's not sin. Don't feel guilty. You're OK. God wouldn't punish you for that." We are asking him or her to give up beliefs about sin, righteousness, God's power to judge, and the path toward forgiveness. Rather, let's say, "If you are feeling guilty, let's pray and ask for God's forgiveness!"

- When we say to a person, "God doesn't want you to have a hard time. Cut this painful situation or this troublesome person out of your life and move forward." God is God within moments of suffering. He may not be the cause of suffering, but can we ever say that He doesn't allow suffering? There's something God is hoping to do in us and through us at all times and in all circumstances. Rather than insist that a person seek out only happy times and happy feelings in his or her faith, let's say, "God is walking with you, working in you, and is going to use this time not only for your good, but for the good of others. I'm here with you, and He's here with both of us. Let's walk forward together."

- When we say to a person, "Take charge of your own life and do what you want to do." No person can truly live an abundant and blessed life apart from God or apart from

His people. We must take into consideration the feelings and position of other people. Rather than encourage people to rebel, or to do what they want to do regardless of others, let's say, "God wants what is best for all His children. He is the master of win-win situations. Let's ask Him what He desires to do not only in your life but in the lives of others."

Job perceived his wife's influence as being discouraging and false. When we perceive that others are attempting to discourage us, or if we have an intuition that they are not speaking God's Word to us, we need to choose not to listen!

Sarah

Sarah is one of the great figures in all the Bible. She was the wife of Abraham, the mother of a miracle baby, Isaac. She was the matriarch of the Hebrew people. She is highly revered and honored as a woman of great courage and faith. But . . . she also gave some very bad advice to her husband. She influenced him in a negative way.

Sarah's intention and motive was good when she came to Abraham and said, "Have a baby by Hagar." Sarah knew that God had promised heirs to her husband and as she saw her own body become incapable of bearing a child, she could not fathom how God was going to fulfill this promise to her husband. It may also have been that Sarah had heard about God's promise for years and years, and she was tired of hearing about it. Either way, Sarah wasn't attempting to disobey God as much as she was trying to help Him out!

After the fruitful Hagar conceived, she began to despise the barren Sarah. And Sarah again attempted to influence her husband—this time to deal harshly with Hagar. Abraham wisely sidestepped the issue and said to Sarah, "Indeed your maid is in your hand; do to her as you please" (Gen. 16:6). So Sarah dealt harshly with Hagar, and Hagar ran away into the wilderness.

An angel spoke to Hagar there, and she eventually returned home and gave birth to Ishmael. Years later, Sarah miraculously conceived and gave birth to Isaac. By the time Isaac was ready to be weaned, probably at the age of three or four, Sarah found Ishmael scoffing at her son. Because Abraham was eighty-six years old when Ishmael was born, and he was one hundred years old when Isaac was born, and at this point it was three or four years later, we can calculate that Ishmael was a young man at this stage, probably near the age of seventeen. Sarah wasn't about to put up with a grown man scoffing at her young son. She perhaps even feared for Isaac's life.

Sarah again went to Abraham to exert her influence. She requested that Hagar and Ishmael be sent away. Abraham didn't want to do this. He loved his older son, and God had given him great promises regarding Ishmael. The Lord spoke to Abraham, and said, "Whatever Sarah has said to you, listen to her voice; for in Isaac your seed shall be called. Yet I will also make a nation of the son of the bondwoman, because he is your seed" (Gen. 21:12b–13). Thus Abraham did as Sarah requested.

Sarah influenced Abraham to conceive Ishmael. Then she influenced Abraham against Hagar. Then she attempted to influence Abraham to send Ishmael and Hagar away.

Is it any wonder that when the time came for Abraham and Isaac to head for Moriah, neither one of them told Sarah? Who can guess what advice she might have given?

For all of Sarah's wonderful, courageous, faithful actions and deeds, she did not influence Abraham well in the matter of his firstborn son. What was her fault?

We have no mention in the Scriptures that Sarah consulted God before advising her husband. In fact, we have no mention that Sarah talked directly with God about anything. God spoke to Sarah through special messengers and He spoke to her through

Abraham. But we have no evidence that Sarah sought out God's advice before she gave her own.

Sarah operated according to her reasoning, her feelings, her fears. She reasoned that Hagar was necessary. She got upset and angry at the way Hagar responded to her once Hagar was pregnant. She feared Ishmael's retaliation or harmful actions against Isaac.

Fear, false reasoning, and feelings of anger or frustration do little to promote sound and righteous influence. In fact, they are poison to it. When a woman is panicked, doesn't have all the facts or hasn't drawn accurate conclusions, or is upset, she should never consult a final decision maker or attempt to exert influence. If she does, she'll likely find that she has just used up her last opportunity to exert good influence, and in turn, she is likely to be even more upset or angry!

Deborah

One of the most influential women in all of Scripture is Deborah. In most cases in the Bible, we find women exerting great influence but not making final decisions. Deborah, however, was a final decision maker.

Deborah called herself a "mother in Israel." (See Judg. 5:7.) Other people called her Judge Deborah.

The Scriptures say she was a prophetess, the wife of Lapidoth, and that she made judgments for the Jewish people while sitting under the palm tree between Ramah and Bethel in the mountains of Ephraim.

One day Deborah sent for Barak, and when he arrived, she said, "Has not the LORD God of Israel commanded, 'Go and deploy troops at Mount Tabor; take with you ten thousand men of the sons of Naphtali and of the sons of Zebulun; and against you I will deploy Sisera, the commander of Jabin's army, with his chariots and his multitude at the River Kishon; and I will deliver him into your hand'?" (Judg. 4:6–7).

Notice the careful way Deborah phrased what she had to say. She says to Barak, in essence, "Don't you already know what the Lord wants you to do?" Deborah made two assumptions: that Barak knew, and that Barak needed only to be reminded. Women often find their advice is taken when they couch their advice in such terms: "Aren't you going to do what it is that you know to do?"

Of course, in the process of asking, Deborah also gave Barak a great deal of information about how many men he was to take, where he was to go, whom he would fight, where the enemy was located, and what the outcome of the battle would be. Deborah was a very wise woman!

I know a woman who is an expert in using this technique. She often makes her point effectively by saying something along these lines: "I know that as you go Christmas shopping, you probably remember that I wear a size 8 in clothes and a size 5 in rings." Or, "Do you think that it would be good for me to wear my pink sweater when we go to the Ryans for dinner at seven o'clock on Friday evening?" Or, "I just hung up your dry cleaning in your closet, so you have a fresh blue shirt to wear with your gray slacks to Kerry's recital tomorrow night."

Even though Deborah was in charge, and both she and Barak knew it, she let Barak make a decision from his own free will. He replied, "If you will go with me, then I will go; but if you will not go with me, I will not go!" (Judg. 4:8). Smart man, but a scared man, too.

Deborah said, "I will surely go with you." She also told him the rest of the story—that there would be no glory for him in the journey because the Lord would defeat Sisera at the hands of a woman.

Barak no doubt thought that Deborah was referring to herself. Nevertheless, he wasn't about to leave for a battle without her.

Barak called the soldiers from Zebulun and Naphtali to

Kedesh. Deborah let him do what he could do, and should have done. She was a judge, not a general, and she didn't attempt to cross that boundary. Sisera arrived on the scene with his nine hundred chariots of iron.

The day for battle came, and Deborah said to Barak, "Up! For this is the day in which the LORD has delivered Sisera into your hand. Has not the LORD gone out before you?" (Judg. 4:14).

Deborah made the final decision. But even as she signaled the start of the battle, she was a source of encouragement to those who would do the fighting. She called them to remember that the Lord was on their side.

When the battle was won, Deborah and Barak sang together a great song of victory. Deborah engineered the battle. Barak and his troops did the fighting. And God gave them the victory. Deborah was generous in including Barak in the exhilaration and fame of the moment.

Job's wife, Sarah, and Deborah teach us that as we exert influence . . .

- We must never seek to turn persons away from their faith in God, or to encourage them to take actions that discount or dismiss God from their lives.
- We must make certain that our information is accurate, our conclusions are reasonable, and our emotions are in check before we seek to exert influence.
- We must not demoralize others as we lead and make decisions, but rather encourage them to believe for God's best in their personal lives and in the lives of others.

....

What About Violent or Radical Means of Influence?

Influence is not passive. It is active and intentional and calls for great wisdom in its execution. And, not all influence in the

Bible is without violence or rebellion—including influence exerted by women.

Let's backtrack to the story of Deborah for a moment. The real hero in this story is neither Deborah nor Barak—it is a woman named Jael.

Jael was Heber's wife, and she is one of those people in the Bible who just happened to be at the right place at the right time. As the enemy general Sisera retreated in his battle against Barak, he was forced to abandon his chariot and flee on foot. He got as far as the tent of Jael, the wife of Heber the Kenite. The king of Hazor and the house of Heber the Kenite had made peace. Jael's tent was located in something of a neutral zone.

Jael greeted Sisera and invited him into her tent, where he collapsed in exhaustion. She covered him with a blanket. Her behavior was in keeping with the unwritten laws of hospitality that are kept to this day by nomadic people in the Middle East. It was not at all unusual for a woman to have her own tent.

Sisera asked for a drink of water, and Jael opened a jug of milk, probably more like a liquid yogurt, and she gave him a drink. She again exhibited great hospitality, going beyond what was requested of her in making a visitor feel welcome. Jael was very shrewd. She gave Sisera no cause to think that he was anything but welcome.

Sisera asked Jael to stand by the entrance to the tent and if anyone came and asked if a man had entered the tent, she was to say "No."

Jael had been kind to Sisera, but he was not her friend, and she was not subject to his orders. She was subject only to the orders of her husband, who may very well have been away from home.

As Sisera fell into a deep sleep, Jael took a tent peg and hammer and moved toward him softly. She got into position and with one mighty blow, she drove the tent peg into his temple and killed him. When Barak showed up at the tent and asked about

Sisera, Jael calmly said to him, "Come, I will show you the man whom you seek."

Nomadic women of that day had the responsibility for tearing down and setting up their own tent homes as they traveled from place to place. They were experts with hammer and peg. Their upper arm muscles were well developed to do just what Jael did. She saw her opportunity to defeat an enemy, and she took it.

We need to keep in mind as we read this story that *Sisera was an enemy*. He was a threat not only to all of Israel, but to Jael's home as well. Had she not invited Sisera into her tent, she would have been subject to his suspicion and perhaps killed. Visitors and travelers had a right to be treated in a hospitable manner. In all likelihood, had Jael resisted or rebuffed Sisera in any way, her life would have been in grave danger. At the same time, for Jael to harbor a man who was not her husband and to let him stay in her tent overnight, would have put her in a bad light. She was in an untenable, dangerous position.

Jael acted in self-defense. There is no indication that she hated Sisera, or that she was thrilled at having killed him. She simply did what she felt she had to do to protect herself and her family. In the process, she protected her entire nation.

Jael's action was violent, but necessary in the moment. Her action was neither premeditated nor was it recommended to others.

Two other women in the Bible took a strong stand—one might even say a rebellious stand—against the leadership over them. Their names were Shiphrah and Puah.

Both were Hebrew midwives. The king of Egypt gave them a command: "When you do the duties of a midwife for the Hebrew women, and see them on the birthstools, if it is a son, then you shall kill him; but if it is a daughter, then she shall live" (Exod. 1:16).

The Scriptures tell us that these two midwives feared God,

and that they did not do as the king of Egypt had commanded them. They kept alive the male children.

When Pharaoh heard what was happening, he called for the midwives and asked them why they had let the male children live. The midwives answered, "Because the Hebrew women are not like the Egyptian women; for they are lively and give birth before the midwives come to them" (Exod. 1:19).

That may or may not have been the case. The Bible isn't clear on that point. It may very well be that Shiphrah and Puah simply made their way very slowly to the homes of women they perceived were going to bear sons. It may be that they delivered male babies and refused to kill them. Either way, they did not obey an evil order.

Now, they didn't incite rebellion in others. They didn't proclaim their own rebellion before others. They simply refused to obey the evil law, knowing full well that their lives were on the line for such disobedience.

This is a critically important point. We cannot refuse to keep the laws of the land, no matter how evil we might regard them, and then expect to be spared from any consequences. If we disobey, we must be willing to pay the penalty for that disobedience, even as we trust God to use our actions to bring about good for our families and nation.

The Bible tells us that God honored these midwives and that He did two things: He allowed the people of Israel to multiply and grow mighty, and He gave the midwives households of their own. In other words, He blessed the midwives with their own children.

Shiphrah and Puah refused to be the puppet executioners of Pharaoh. They insisted that if he wanted evil done, he do it himself.

Is it right to rebel against the laws of the land? Apparently, yes, on an individual level and if a person is fully willing to accept the full consequences of her actions.

Is it ever right to use violent means against one's enemies? Apparently, yes, as a matter of self-defense.

....

The Great Importance of Family and Nation

One of the things to note about the power to influence is that each of the *righteous* women mentioned in this chapter exerted her influence for the good of her *family*.

A woman has every right, scripturally speaking, to defend her family, speak up on behalf of her family, plead for her family, and do whatever it takes to ensure her family's safety, welfare, and joy—physically, materially, and spiritually.

None of the righteous women cited in this chapter defended a cause or a law. None of them fought for the right of an organization or an institution. None of them sought retribution against enemies, except as it brought protection or preservation of her family. Each of them had the family as her primary concern. All of them were masterful in their influence and their efforts brought great reward, which went far beyond their immediate families.

Just because we might focus our efforts on a highly personal or localized concern does not mean that our efforts won't have widespread impact. We have seen a number of instances of this in recent years—for example, the woman who defended her son's right to attend school even though he had HIV, and the woman who was willing to go to jail rather than allow her daughter to be abused by the girl's father. These women were not defending a cause. They were defending their children. And yet, their defense had great impact on national discussion and ultimately, on certain policy decisions.

The Bible places great importance on families. The immediate family was of greatest concern to a Bible woman, and then beyond the immediate family, her concern was extended to the larger circle of family members, which in Bible times became the tribe or even the nation. All Hebrew people considered themselves to be related. National concerns were essentially family concerns!

How does this apply to you? What is threatening your family? What is attempting to destroy the fabric of your home life? That matter should be your primary concern. Make it a matter of prayer and thought. What can you do to enhance the spiritual peace and the eternal preservation of your husband, children, parents, or other relatives? What is at stake? What are the consequences if you don't take action?

The urgency of your problem will set the timetable for your action. The depth of the feeling you have will impact your perseverance in getting the job done. The more personal the problem, the greater your passion will be about it, and the more potent your influence will be.

Look at the mirror of your own life, especially as it relates to the lives of your family members. Look at your children, spouse, and parents. What is threatening them?

Then, look around you to see who can help you change the situation or can bring about the solution you seek. Go to that person for help. It may be a man or woman. The person may be a political leader, a community leader, or a person of financial means. In some cases it may even be you! Go privately to those whose help you seek. They are less likely to be threatened and more likely to hear you out fully.

Map out a strategy. What must you do to gain access to this person? What preparations do you need to make? Above all, talk to the Lord about what it is that He would have you do.

There's a great deal that can and should be done to bring about positive change in our world today. Begin with your family concerns, set a goal and determine who can help you get there, map out a strategy for presenting your concern to this person, and put your plan into gear.

....

Choosing the Best Influencing Technique

Virtually any of the powers can be used along with influence. Often a woman's first and foremost choice is to choose the most effective means of influencing available to her. An example of this came home to me recently.

Once while I was out of town, two of my friends marched in an anti-abortion, pro-life rally. They were unprepared for the violent opposition they received. Although nearly 200 women marched in the pro-life lines and only a dozen or so in the pro-choice line, the news media covered the two groups as if they were equal in size. Personal insults were hurled in only one direction—from pro-choicers toward pro-lifers. When I asked my friends what they thought they had accomplished, they replied, "Actually, very little. A few people may have seen our signs and thought twice." Overall, they were very frustrated and felt anything but powerful and influential.

I shared with them the experiences of two women I had met while speaking. One of them, Karen, was the wife of a hospital administrator. She learned that abortions were conducted at the hospital where her husband worked. She quietly did her research and one day she made an appointment to meet with her husband in his office at the hospital. She presented her husband with a ten-page document that she and two of her friends had prepared over a two-month period. The document presented a number of scientific arguments and statistics, including the number of abortions conducted in her husband's hospital. She recommended that the hospital change its policy providing for abortions on demand.

Karen wisely anticipated some of the objections her husband might raise and presented cogent, fact-based answers. She neither raised her voice nor used unfair tactics. After a half hour, she rose and said, "Thank you for hearing me out on this," and left. She never brought up the subject at home.

Several weeks later, her husband came home and handed her a copy of a document for her to see. It stated a revision of the hospital's policy about abortions, and was signed by the chairman of the hospital's board of directors.

Another woman, Mayse, told me about what a group of women in her church had decided to do regarding the abortion issue. These women weren't much for marching or sitting on clinic steps in protest. Rather, Mayse said, they opted to influence primarily the young women in their church.

She and two of her friends began their campaign of influence by asking for the privilege of presenting a program to the foremost women's organization in their church. During the program they outlined what was currently *not* being taught to their daughters and young women in the church about sex, contraception, and abortion. At the close of their program, they asked the women's group to sponsor a workshop for girls twelve and older in their church. The all-day workshop they proposed, which would be attended voluntarily and be free of charge, included a number of sessions on contraception, abstinence before marriage, the wonders of childbirth, Bible references about children, and facts related to abortion. The women's group wholeheartedly supported this program. Once the women's group had given their support, the senior pastor quickly gave his support.

To the surprise of the women, nearly a hundred teens and pre-teens showed up for the workshop. Almost half of those in attendance were friends of the young women in their church. The young women responded favorably to the presentation, which included a film and several guest speakers, one of whom had had an abortion and regretted that decision.

The interest was so great that a second workshop was held six months later. The women now plan to sponsor their "motherhood" workshop once a year. Mayse knows of at least three young women who opted not to have an abortion after being influenced by one of the teens who attended the workshop—a good result from positive peer pressure! She and the other women of her church believe that none of the young women who attend their workshops will ever abort a child.

Do Karen and Mayse feel influential? Very much so!

What are you to do about moral issues impacting your community and the nation? The answer is to train! (See chapter 6.) In my opinion, training is the appropriate avenue of power for debate, discussion, information sharing, and other forms of "teaching" that can most effectively impact policy and legal issues. Influence whenever you can, and train whenever possible. This is a both/and, not an either/or situation.

Part of having power as a woman is knowing which techniques work best in which situations!

Exerting Influence in the Kingdom of God

Here, again, are the key principles that we see in Bible women about the exertion of influential power:

- Thorough advance preparation
- Operating through channels, in the fullness of position, and according to protocol
- Giving before requesting
- Speaking from personal concern and out of personal and family need
- Having boldness in naming the enemy when asked
- Not allowing fear, false reasoning, anger, or frustration to enter the process of influence
- Leaving room for the final decision maker to act out of his or her own free will, without sensing coercion or threat
- Refusing to undermine a person's belief in or reliance upon God

- Encouraging and believing for God's best while exerting influence or making decisions

Refer to this criteria and ask, Is there a need to be filled within your local church body? Is there a community need that your church should address?

Remember, from a scriptural standpoint, God's people in your local church are part of your spiritual family.

One woman I know saw a problem in her child's Sunday school. She concluded that her daughter was not being taught the Scriptures, but rather, was being asked to tackle moral issues and community concerns from a perspective of moral relativism and social action. She firmly believed that church was the place to learn the Bible. She felt that the present and future spiritual life of her child was at stake.

This woman began exerting her influence by writing down in comprehensive detail what she thought a good elementary church school curriculum should entail. And then, she thoroughly researched alternate curricula that other churches of her denomination were using, as well as a couple of programs churches within her neighborhood were using. She found one curriculum in particular that she liked, and that she felt met all the criteria she had listed.

Next, she talked to several parents whose children were participating in the curriculum of her choice. She also made an appointment with the Sunday school leader who supervised the curriculum. The Sunday school leader mentioned to her that a seminar about this particular curriculum was being conducted in a city just an hour's drive away.

This woman gave careful thought as to whom she should approach in her own church. She knew that the church's present Christian education director was new in her position, and that she had not made the decision about the present curriculum. That decision had been made by her predecessor. She asked enough discreet questions to learn that the Christian education director had the authority to adopt new curriculum materials, that a budget was allocated for this purpose, and that the clergy members to whom the director reported were not vitally committed to any particular curriculum.

This woman then went to the director of Christian education and invited the director to explore this particular curriculum with her at the seminar in the nearby city. She paid for the trip and seminar fees and treated the Christian education director to a lovely lunch on the way. As they traveled to the seminar, she asked the director about her approach and ideas. On the way home, she suggested that if the Christian education director had questions, the director might contact the person at the church whom the woman had visited several weeks earlier. When the Christian education director asked her if she would volunteer to teach Sunday school if this new curriculum was adopted, she agreed.

The woman didn't press, coerce, or pressure the Christian education director in any way. She didn't put together a coalition of parents or make a big fuss within the church. She didn't campaign for her cause. In fact, she didn't even discuss her efforts with anyone other than her husband.

Two weeks later the Christian education director called the woman to say that the church was going to adopt the curriculum they had previewed together, and she thanked this woman for bringing it to her attention.

I feel certain that nobody in that particular church knows what brought about the change in curriculum materials. Most of the parents are probably not aware that their children are now students in a more Bible-based program. God knows. This one woman knows. And the children will benefit as the result.

What this woman probably doesn't realize is that because her particular church is influential in her denomination, several other churches in her city and state have taken her church's switch in curriculum as a signal that they should consider a similar switch! The domino effect of five or six churches making such a switch in a two-year period caused at least one national publishing house to sit up and take notice.

This woman had no intention of causing a national movement. She was simply concerned that her eight-year-old daughter have a more Bible-based Sunday school experience. Nevertheless, she exerted great influence—quietly, unobtrusively, but oh so effectively!

What do you want to see changed? Make a plan for exerting your influence toward that goal. You have the power to do so!

3

....

The
Power to
Seduce

Women have the power to seduce.

When I have made that statement to various groups of women over the past several years, I have observed that women tend to react in one of two ways. Most smile, slightly raise their eyebrows, and give a "knowing" glance to the person sitting next to them. A few become very tight-lipped, as if this is something that women shouldn't talk about in polite company.

Both reactions indicate to me that virtually all women are convinced that women have this power, themselves included! Nobody ever gives me a puzzled, I-don't-have-the-foggiest-idea-what-you-are-talking-about look.

The word *seduce* has several different meanings, but in this chapter it means "to attract."Females are seducers from an early age. Just watch a three-year-old girl at "work" in a room with men. If Dad or Grandpa is in the room, she's likely to get from them just about anything she wants.

If little boys are in the room, she will flirt, but only with the ones with whom she wants to play. Her stance, her smile, her looks of approval and affection—you can't convince me that women aren't born capable of seducing men.

And of course, the techniques that work on Dad and Grandpa rarely work on Mom and Grandma. Why? Because Mom and Grandma have been there. They're wise to the techniques and can't be swayed so easily. A little girl uses an entirely different set of techniques when she seeks to get something she wants from an older female.

Most women, however, have been taught that seduction, for a variety of reasons, is bad.

It can be. But it need not be.

Seduction is a technique of power—a type of power that is essentially neutral. The motivation for seducing, whether intentional or unintentional, is what determines whether the seduction is evil or righteous. The same holds for the choice of person being seduced and the end being sought.

As a technique, seduction has three steps. All of them are clearly presented in the story of Adam and Eve in the Garden of Eden.

....

Eve, a Victim of Seduction

A great many women seem to think that Eve was a seducer. The Bible account doesn't automatically lead to that conclusion. Rather, we are told that Eve and Adam were of "one flesh." As such, they so completely complemented each other that the action of one was as the action of the other. Eve no more would have thought of doing something to harm Adam, or to entice him to do something evil, than she would have done something to harm herself.

In fact, there's not even a hint that Eve had to entice Adam in any way. She needed to give Adam no information and no encouragement to eat of the forbidden fruit. Why not? Because, unlike many of the pictures we see in children's Bible storybooks, Adam was not off in another part of the Garden while Eve was engaging in her conversation with the serpent. The Scriptures say that he was "with her," silently assenting to what was said and done, until the moment when he partook of the fruit for himself. Adam wasn't taken for a ride. He was along for the ride. Adam and Eve fell together into disobedience.

The real seducer in the Garden of Eden story is the serpent, who is described as being "more cunning than any beast of the field which the LORD God had made" (Gen. 3:1). It is from the serpent that we see the pattern of seduction.

The Serpent Gets Eve's Attention

He asks her a general question. Eve doesn't have even a hint as to the direction the serpent is intending to take in the conversation. The serpent asks only, "Has God indeed said, 'You shall not eat of every tree of the garden'?" Eve responds by saying, in essence, "Yes, that's what God said. We can eat of every tree except the one in the middle of the garden. If we eat of that one, or even touch it, we will die." (See Gen. 3:1–3.) The first step of any seduction is: Get attention.

The Serpent Offers Eve Secret Information

The clear implication of his next remark is that he knows something about God that Eve doesn't know. He says, "You will not surely die. For God knows that in the day you eat of it your eyes will be opened, and you will be like God, knowing good and evil" (Gen. 3:4–5).

This interests Eve, of course, because with all of her being, she longs to be more like God, her Creator. Her desire is to be one with Him, just as she is one with Adam. That's the built-in desire of all human beings—total identification with their Maker. The second step of seduction is: Present to the person the idea that you know something, or have something, that he or she doesn't know or have, but would like to know or have.

To a great extent, the strength of the seduction lies at this point more than at the first or third stages. The person must already intuitively want what the seducer is trying to sell. He or she is willing to take a risk to get the information or object because it is something perceived as good and desirable for his or her personal welfare.

We have no indication in the Scriptures that Eve thought she was gambling with her life and future. There's every indication, on the other hand, that Eve thought she was doing something that would make her even more like God, whom she loved, and that the newfound knowledge would be for her benefit.

We also have no indication that Eve was operating on impulse, against reason or logic—that she was being a gullible, "emotional" woman in her decision making.

Consider what Eve knew about life and death at that point. Eve knew that she had access to the tree of life. God had not forbidden her, or Adam, to eat of the fruit of that particular tree, which was also located in the middle of the Garden. She knew God had made a provision for her to live. The serpent's words that she would not surely die made logical sense to her. It was not an emotional appeal. It was an appeal rooted in logic and reason. *After all*, Eve may have thought, *God has given us the tree of life, so indeed, we probably won't die. The serpent may have a point here. Perhaps he does know something about God that I don't know. Perhaps this serpent is actually God's messenger so that I will come into wisdom. Perhaps the rule only applied to me until I had matured to this point where I was capable of discerning good from evil.*

The Serpent Lets Eve Survey the Situation

He doesn't press the fruit of the tree into her hand or force-feed it to her. He allows her just enough space to take another look at the tree and its fruit, and to think about the situation. The partaking of the forbidden fruit is not a matter of impulse buying. Eve looks, studies, decides, and then she takes of the fruit and eats, sharing with Adam as she does. The third step of seduction is: Give the person something highly appealing to look at and think about.

....

The Three Steps of Seduction

The three steps of seduction have been used by both men and women through the centuries, whether to sell toothpaste, to win an agreeable sexual partner for the night, or to gain financial security and social status.

1. Get Attention

Consider the woman in the supermarket who sees a handsome guy without a wedding band struggling to decide which cantaloupe to buy. She asks a simple question, "Do you know how farmers tell when cantaloupes are ripe?" An innocent opening line.

Consider the young woman who lays her trap, carefully monitoring the movements of the guy in her history class whom she wants as her date for the Christmas banquet. She just happens to be standing in the right place at the right time to say, "I noticed you weren't in class last Wednesday. Did you get notes from the lecture?" He never suspects.

Consider the five-year-old girl who hangs upside down on the monkey bars and makes a face and then asks her targeted guy, "Can you hang upside down on the monkey bars like this?" Sure he can, and surely he will. And just as surely, he's snagged.

2. Give the Hint of "More" Available for the Asking

The appeal here is to basic desires: pride, companionship, physical appetite, sexual lust, greed, thirst for knowledge, quest for power, search for fame.

For instance, the woman in the supermarket may say, "I love cantaloupe. Have you ever had half a cantaloupe with a big scoop of French vanilla ice cream?" The hint is there—I know even more about cantaloupe than how to determine if one is ripe for eating. Wouldn't you like for me to teach you more, and in the process, feed you dessert?

Or she might take a quick survey of the guy's supermarket cart and say, "All those fast foods. When was the last time you had a real home-cooked meal?" Or, "I can tell you're really into wholesome eating. Have you ever been to the nutrition store on Fifty-first Street?" A bat of the lashes doesn't hurt. He may not respond, but it's not for a lack of trying.

The young woman anxious for a date to the Christmas banquet may ask, "Are you ready for next Friday's test?" The hint is: I have good notes. I'm looking for a study partner. Wouldn't you like to study with me, and in the process, get a better grade and make a new friend? Or perhaps she tries, "I know you are a serious student and I'd hate to see you not have good notes as you study for next week's exam." Thus, she sends the signal, "You need more of what I have to offer."

Five-year-olds cut to the chase fairly quickly. "Would you like to come to my birthday party next Saturday?" She has a party to offer, probably with cake and ice cream.

3. Give Something to Look At and Think About

Whether revealing an ankle or wearing a low-cut neckline, women have been masters for centuries of giving men just a little more to look at and think about.

Part of a woman's art of seduction is giving a man a little time to ponder before she makes her next call or appearance. The act the woman undertakes need not be overtly sexual or physical. She might bake a cake and surprise him with it. She might write a special note of encouragement and leave it in his locker the afternoon before the big game. She might stand up for him when the other kids start to tease him.

The man is left thinking, *This is a good woman. I like what she does for me. I need to spend a little more time around her.*

....

Seduction and Sexual Arousal Differ

Seduction can include or lead to sexual arousal. But not all seduction leads to that end. And not all sexual arousal occurs as the result of seduction.

Men are hormonally "engineered" in such a way that it doesn't take a genuine act of seduction for them to be ready, willing, and eager for sexual activity. In some cases, a sensuous cue might be all it takes to cause a man to become sexually aroused.

In the case of Delilah, sexual arousal and seduction are closely linked. Perhaps no other story has influenced us more in our associating seduction with sex. (See Judges 16.)

Delilah's real motivation, however, was not sex. It was money. She had been hired by a group of Philistines to discover the source of Samson's great power. If she succeeded, she would be paid several thousand dollars in today's monetary value.

Samson wanted love. From earlier stories in the book of Judges, we see that Samson fell hard and fast for women. He was an easy mark. He had judged Israel for twenty years, which means that he was not a young man when he met Delilah. In fact, he may very well have been at the midlife crisis stage. Whatever his situation, the Bible says he "loved a woman in the Valley of Sorek, whose name was Delilah." Samson wanted a loving relationship.

The story of Samson and Delilah begins after they have already developed some sort of relationship. We infer this, in part, because the story in the Bible immediately preceding this one is about Samson's experience with a harlot, and the ambush that was attempted against him after a one-night stand with her. Delilah is not called a harlot, and Samson apparently is committed to her to some degree because he is with her for longer than a day or two.

Delilah no doubt admired Samson's great physical strength. She probably told him on more than one occasion, "You're so big and so strong." So Samson probably didn't think it was unusual when Delilah inquired about the secret to his strength.

Samson told Delilah that if she bound him with seven fresh bowstrings, he'd be weak and just like other men. It's difficult for me to imagine that Samson would have told Delilah this unless he fully expected her to tie him up so he could, in turn, show her his great strength.

When Delilah cried, "The Philistines are upon you, Samson!" she knew the Philistines were hiding in the room. But Samson didn't know it, and he broke the bonds easily. There is no indication that the Philistines revealed themselves.

Again, Delilah went after Samson's secret. This time he said that if he was bound with new ropes, he would become weak. Another game. Another opportunity to show off to his beloved. And again, when Delilah said, "The Philistines are upon you, Samson!" Samson broke the bonds and the Philistines remained in hiding.

When Delilah went after Samson's secret a third time, Samson told her he could be bound if she weaved seven strands of his hair into the web of a loom. But again he was only joking with her. Finally, Delilah said to Samson, "How can you say, 'I love you,' when your heart is not with me? You have mocked me these three times, and have not told me where your great strength lies" (Judg. 16:15).

From this verse, we can conclude that Samson had told Delilah on a number of occasions that he loved her. Delilah tried to manipulate Samson when she said, in effect, "You say you love me, but you never talk to me. You never share your secrets with me."

A note here on manipulation. Manipulation is rooted in a lie. Remember, Delilah wanted money from the Philistines. She claimed to want information to further her love relationship with Samson, when in fact, she wanted information to end their relationship. She was dishonest with Samson about what she truly wanted.

Seduction can be used for manipulation, but all seduction is not manipulation. Seduction is using attention-getting, enticing, and timing techniques to get something—but that something need not be rooted in a lie. Manipulation is never acceptable to God.

How can you tell the difference?

Very simply. If a person says to you, "Are you attempting to seduce me?" you must answer, "Yes." If the person asks, "Why are you trying to seduce me?" you must give an honest answer. You must be willing at all times in an "honest" seduction to reveal not only what you are doing, but why.

We don't know how many more times Delilah asked Samson the source of his strength, but apparently she did ask more than these four times. The implication is that she wore out Samson playing this game. Judges 16:16 says, "she pestered him daily with her words and pressed him, so that his soul was vexed to death." Delilah played the game until Samson was out of energy, out of inventive games, and ultimately, at least to a degree, out of his mind. He told her the truth: "If I am shaven, then my strength will leave me."

Delilah lulled Samson to sleep. She cradled him and soothed him until he collapsed into her lap, completely spent. And then she shaved off the seven locks of his head. This time when she awoke him, saying, "The Philistines are upon you, Samson!" Samson no longer had strength, and indeed, the Philistines *were* upon him. They put out his eyes, bound him with bronze fetters, and hauled him to prison.

Delilah's manipulative seduction of Samson was linked to sexual arousal. Hers was an entirely *intentional* manipulation.

I don't believe most women are as calculating and manipulative as Delilah. The far greater likelihood is that women tease and seduce without knowing that they are arousing a man sexually. They think they are innocently flirting, not engaging in foreplay. They think they are merely teasing, not intending to provoke sexual desire.

It's the innocent, unintentional seduction that gets many women, including many teenagers, into situations where a man *thinks* the woman has said yes to sex, even though that wasn't remotely what she intended. Women should be aware and guard against these nonverbal cues that men may misinterpret.

From what I have observed and from discussions I have had with numerous women about seduction, I have concluded that most women engage in the three stages of seduction without even thinking about them. They are an intuitive part of the way a woman functions. Rarely does a woman need to calculate or ponder the process.

And in that lies the potential for great danger.

....

Seduction As an Intentional Act of Power

Women have the power to seduce men, and they sometimes seduce men without even meaning to do so.

Certainly that happened to Bathsheba. There is no indication in the Scriptures that she *intended* to seduce David. She was innocently bathing late one evening when David was walking on the roof of his house and he spotted her. It was a chance viewing, but David was smitten nonetheless.

Many a woman has attracted suitors without any intention of doing so. Even if she gives thought to what she might have done or said, she will most likely conclude, "I didn't do anything." Which is more accurately stated, "I didn't intend to do anything." Just by being herself—by caring, showing concern, being beautiful, appearing vulnerable—she may have gained the attention of a man.

As adult women, we need to warn our daughters about this possibility. How many young women today wear clothing, makeup, and hairstyles that belie their true age and level of innocence, only to become puzzled and annoyed because the guys won't leave them alone? Although they may not consciously "ask" to be noticed, wooed, and pursued, they are asking nonetheless.

Herodias's daughter didn't have a clue, at least as far as we are told in the Gospel of Mark, as to what she was doing to King Herod when she danced before him. Like so many young women in her time, she had been taught to dance and she loved to dance. The pretty clothes, the music, the freedom of movement, the privilege of being invited to the party were all fun and exciting for her, just as they are to many women today. She danced at Herod's birthday feast, and her dance "pleased" Herod.

We have no way of knowing how old this young woman was. She may have been only a girl. She may have been a teenager. And, we don't know in what way she pleased Herod. Was he proud of her for the way she danced in front of his friends? Was he sexually aroused? Was he just showing off for his friends after a wonderful performance? The Scriptures don't say. We do know, however, that he was so pleased and was feeling so good on his birthday, that he made a grand gesture, saying, "Whatever you ask me, I will give you, up to half my kingdom" (Mark 6:23).

And the daughter of Herodias didn't know what to say.

This situation is quite common in today's world. The guy in the shiny black car offers a woman a seat next to him so that she can join him in cruising down Main Street. A man offers a woman a trip to his condo at the lake for an out-of-town weekend. A boy asks a girl to go fishing with him on Saturday. The stranger walks across the restaurant to ask a woman for her phone number or if she will join him for dessert.

And women don't know what to say. There was no intention to seduce so quickly, so easily. And suddenly, a woman no longer feels in control. It happens to women all the time, and at even younger and younger ages.

Herodias's daughter ran to her mother and said, "What shall I ask?" This young woman may have had in mind a new gold necklace or bracelet, or a lovely silk scarf, or perhaps even a camel or two of her own to ride with her friends. Her mother, however, had something far more sinister in mind. She wanted the head of John the Baptist on a platter. And this young woman didn't even think twice before returning to Herod and requesting her mother's wish.

A daughter will respond to men the way her mother teaches her to respond. She may not know she is seducing, and she may be surprised to discover that she has, but when the man responds with an offer of his own, she needs to know what to say! The response she gives is going to be the one her mother or guardian has taught her to give.

Mothers should teach their daughters how to respond. They should talk openly to their daughters or the young women whom they influence about the natural seducing power that a young woman has. It won't work to tell her *not* to seduce. It's part of her inborn power as a female. Rather, she should learn how to seduce in positive ways . . . how to seduce the right people at the right times . . . and how to seduce for noble purposes.

....
Who Is Worthy of a Woman's Seduction?

The person worthy of a woman's sexual seduction is the man she intends to spend the rest of her life seducing.

God didn't intend for seduction to be a one-time action. He intended for it to be part of a lifetime relationship.

If you are married, the man you are to seduce is your

husband. And if you aren't married, the man you are to seduce is the one you intend to make your husband.

Leah knew that she wasn't Jacob's first choice for a wife. Nevertheless, because of the customs of the day, she became his first wife. She had him to herself only for a week, and then her younger sister Rachel became part of her life forever. We are told very plainly in the Scriptures that Leah was "unloved" by Jacob. (See Genesis 29–30.)

Still, Jacob fulfilled his obligation to her as a husband. With Jacob, Leah conceived children. After her first son, Reuben, was born she said, "Now therefore, my husband will love me" (Gen. 29:32*b*). Not so. After the birth of Simeon she said, "Because the LORD has heard that I am unloved, He has therefore given me this son also" (v. 33).

She had a third son, Levi, and again she said, "Now this time my husband will become attached to me, because I have borne him three sons" (v. 34). Still not so.

By the time Leah had her fourth son, she apparently had given up on gaining Jacob's love because she says in response to the birth of Judah, "Now I will praise the LORD" (v. 35).

And she temporarily stopped bearing.

Rachel's maid Bilhah bore the next two sons to Jacob—Dan and Naphtali. Leah's maid Zilpah bore sons seven and eight, Gad and Asher.

At this point in the Bible narrative, Leah's oldest son went into the wheat harvest and found mandrakes, believed to be an aphrodisiac, and he brought them home to his mother. Rachel begged to have some of them but Leah refused. Why? Leah intended to seduce her husband.

Leah met Jacob as he came out of the field in the evening, and she said, "Come to my tent tonight. I have mandrakes."

And sure enough, she got his attention. Jacob was intrigued that she had something "more" to offer him, and that night, Leah conceived her fifth son, Issachar. And in the following years, she bore him a sixth son, Zebulun, and a daughter she named Dinah.

In all, Leah "seduced" her husband Jacob into giving her seven children—six of them sons—and as the story turns out, they became half of all the tribes of Israel. Bilhah, Zilpah, and eventually Rachel had two sons each.

Leah knew she wasn't loved. In fact, love seems to have had no role in her relationship with Jacob. But she continued to seduce her husband nonetheless. She made herself available to him and got his attention. She held out a promise of "something more" to him over the course of many years and even after it appeared that she could have no more children. She never made his decisions for him, but she broadly hinted at what she desired from him.

In the end, Leah outlived her sister Rachel by many years. Rachel died after giving birth to her second son, Benjamin. Leah, the unloved, was buried by her husband in the same place that Abraham, Sarah, Isaac, and Rebekah were buried. It was in this place that Jacob intended to be buried someday. (See Gen. 49:29–31.)

Leah knew something that many women today seem to have forgotten: A wife needs to keep seducing her husband all of his life, because if she doesn't, somebody else will.

How many men have been seduced away from their wives because another woman got their attention—asked for their advice or help—and then offered them something more than what they were already getting at home? How many women have heard their husbands say to them, "I've found someone new."

Wives, *keep getting your husband's attention*. Try the new recipe. Wear the new outfit. Find the new interesting thing to talk about. Pursue the new venture together.

One of the finest compliments I have ever heard a man make about his wife was this comment from a national church leader, who said with a smile, "I never know what my wife is going to come up with next." She had his full attention and believe me, no other woman on the planet was given a chance to catch his eye.

Wives, *stay interesting to your husbands*. A man who thinks he knows everything there is to know about his wife will quickly become bored with her. I've heard several men who have been married more than fifty years say, with great pleasure, "I'm still learning new things about my wife every day."

One of the best ways a woman can stay interesting to her husband is to find out what interests the husband and then do those things, learn about those things, and contribute to his understanding of those things. Men may not want to admit that they take advice from their wives, but they nearly always do. That advice is often more palatable to them when it is couched in terms of "I read an interesting article today" or "I heard a program today" or "I learned today" statements.

A wife should give her husband just enough space to miss the good things she does for him. That space might be an occasional day away with friends, or the opportunity for him to see her across the room engaged in conversation with other people. It might be the space of refusing to nag him any further about a particular issue. One woman I know gives her husband space by saying, "Let me present something for your consideration and decision," and then she fully states her case. She waits a full three days before she raises the issue again by asking, "Have you thought about my idea (or request)?" (She considers three days enough time for any idea to be in the tomb before it is resurrected!)

Another woman used this technique for more than forty-five years in her marriage: "Honey, I want to go to California for the Christmas holidays, and I'm going to fight fair. I'm telling you right now that I'm going to do everything in my power to convince you to go." She always said this with a smile, knowing that he had no desire to spend the holidays with her family and away from his workshop. And then for the next six weeks, he found himself eating all of his favorite meals and receiving many nice surprises. There's no way he could ever have said no to her when the time came to purchase the airline tickets! He was properly, thoroughly, and delightfully seduced into a California Christmas year after year.

....

Being a Righteous Seductress

Two women rarely called "seductresses" are Ruth and Naomi. Nevertheless, they belong in that classification.

In a wonderful expression of loyalty and love, Ruth refused to stay behind in Moab when Naomi decided to return to her homeland after the death of her husband and sons, one of whom was Ruth's husband. Ruth clung to her mother-in-law and said, "Wherever you go, I will go; and wherever you lodge, I will lodge; your people shall be my people, and your God, my God. Where you die, I will die, and there will I be buried" (Ruth 1:16–17).

The two of them traveled to Bethlehem and were warmly greeted by Naomi's friends there. It was the time of the barley harvest, and Ruth asked Naomi if she could go to glean wheat in the field of one of Naomi's kinsmen, a man by the name of Boaz. She desired to go so that she might win this man's favor. (See Ruth 2:2.) Naomi agreed.

Ruth wanted more than grain. She desired to be liked by the owner of the field. She intended to do such a fine job that she would be noticed and appreciated, and through that, gain a place for her mother-in-law and herself. In other words, Ruth intended to get the attention of Boaz.

She succeeded. Boaz noticed the new young woman among the gleaners who were following the reapers. He asked who she was and he watched her work. He noticed that she worked from early morning, resting only occasionally.

Ruth asked only for the privilege of gleaning and nothing more. But Boaz responded by saying, "Don't work in anybody else's field. Stay close by my young women who are in the field. When you are thirsty, drink from the vessels that I've provided."

Ruth responded, "Why should I have such favor in your eyes, since I am a foreigner?" She wanted his favor but did not presume that she would automatically gain it. Boaz replied, "It has been fully reported to me, all that you have done for your mother-in-law since the death of your husband, and how you have left your father and your mother and the land of your birth, and have come to a people whom you did not know before." And then he added, "The LORD repay your work, and a full reward be given you by the LORD God of Israel, under whose wings you have come for refuge" (Ruth 2:11–12).

Ruth thanked Boaz for his kind words and told him that she sought to earn his favor.

During the midday mealtime, Boaz invited Ruth to sit with him and partake of the bread, vinegar, and parched grain they were having as a meal. She did, and then she went immediately back to glean.

Ruth had Boaz's attention. She said just enough to intrigue him into wanting to know more. And she gave him space to consider her presence.

Ruth gleaned until evening and returned to her mother-in-law at their place of lodging in the city. When she gave a report of the day's events to Naomi, Naomi offered her advice to further the seduction. She said, "This man is a relation of ours, one of our close relatives" (v. 20). And then Naomi presented a bold plot for Ruth to follow in completing her seduction of Boaz. The intent was a good one, especially in that age and culture, so that Ruth would have security and so that neither woman would be forced into prostitution.

Ruth followed Naomi's advice. She washed herself and anointed herself, put on her best garment, and went down to the threshing floor, where she hid herself in the shadows until Boaz finished eating and drinking and lay down to sleep for the night. It was then that Ruth drew close to him, uncovered his feet, and lay down, in essence, at the foot of his bed.

In actuality, this is an extremely suggestive, sexual move. For a single woman to lie down at the foot of a wealthy landowner, uncover his feet, and then warm his feet with her own body, strongly suggests, "Take me, I'm yours." There's no more seductive and yet honest, non-manipulative action that Ruth could have taken, and she knew it. She put all of her eggs into this basket. If Boaz shunned her, the word would spread quickly throughout Bethlehem. If he accepted her, she would be spared.

Furthermore, Ruth left nothing to chance or Boaz's goodwill. She iced the cake by looking and smelling her best, and wearing her best dress.

At midnight, Boaz suddenly awoke and was startled to find a woman lying at his feet. He spoke to her in the darkness, "Who are you?" And Ruth responded, "I am Ruth, your maidservant. Take your maidservant under your wing, for you are a close relative" (Ruth 3:9). Ruth asked for what she wanted, but she didn't demand it.

Everything about her behavior was alluring, gracious, and desirable in Boaz's eyes. He said, "Blessed are you of the LORD, my daughter! For you have shown more kindness at the end than at the beginning, in that you did not go after young men, whether poor or rich" (v. 10).

Boaz felt flattered that Ruth had come to him and that she desired to be with him. He felt honored by her presence. He had been thoroughly, delightfully, and rightly seduced.

Boaz "redeemed" Ruth the next day according to the customs of the land, and he made her his wife. The son she bore, Obed, had a son named Jesse, who in turn had a son named David. David became king of all Israel, and was an ancestor of

Jesus. The foreign woman, Ruth, seduced her way right into the lineage of the Messiah.

·······················

Principles of Righteousness

Seduction is a righteous use of power when it follows these principles:

1. The person being seduced is "lawful" to be seduced. Seduction is never right if it involves immorality of any kind. For a woman to seduce another woman's husband is adultery. For a woman to seduce a man into sexual immorality prior to marriage is fornication. Both are expressly forbidden in God's Word.

For a woman to set her sights on a man who is of legal age, is single, and is available for marriage—having made no other commitments or taken any other vows that preclude his being married—is acceptable in God's eyes, according to God's Word.

All other purposes apart from marriage need to be weighed against God's Word.

2. The motivation is to achieve an end that is right in God's eyes. Marriage is permitted, and blessed, by God. For a person to desire to be married is normal and acceptable according to God's Word.

In the realm of nonsexual seduction, honest business partnerships and relationships are acceptable. So are friendships. The conversion of lost souls is not only honorable, but also commanded.

3. The means of seduction do not involve immorality, trickery, or deceit. The seducer must be willing to admit openly and honestly his or her motives and intended goal. The seducer must not lie to achieve the goal, and thus, must not engage in manipulation.

The use of drugs and alcohol is not acceptable. The person must not be deluded or tricked in any way into accepting a proposition.

Enticement is not trickery. Enticement is making something as appealing and desirable as possible. It is presenting the best possible face, or as in Ruth's case, taking a bath, anointing the body, and wearing the best garments. These actions say to the other person, "I want to do you a legitimate favor, and I'm going to do my best to convince you to accept what I genuinely believe is best for both of us."

....

Using the Power of Seduction to Enhance the Kingdom of God

The three principles regarding righteous seduction and the three techniques of seduction described earlier are presented in a summary format below:

Techniques	Right Use
Get attention	"Lawful" person being seduced
Hint at more	Moral end goal
Provide memorable "gift"	No trickery or deceit

Let's apply these techniques and principles to the expansion and enhancement of God's kingdom here on earth. In so doing, we are joining forces with the One who woos men and women to Christ, the Holy Spirit. The Scriptures say that the Spirit gently, persistently, and lovingly woos us to Christ. The Spirit brings Christ to our attention. The Spirit presents Christ in His fullness, which is to make Him appealing and compelling. The Spirit lets us make our decision about Christ, never demanding or giving ultimatums, but also never relenting or abandoning the Father's heartfelt desire to nurture us, care for us, and love us as His children and heirs of His promise.

Even after we have accepted Christ as our Savior and Lord, the Holy Spirit continues to draw us ever closer to Christ. We are chastened at times, and yet even in those moments, we are chastened *with love*. The Father's desire is that we be ever more like Christ, and be in an ever-growing and ever-deepening relationship with Him.

The Holy Spirit woos us all of our lives, continually drawing us upward in spirit and outward in our expressions of love to others, until we reach our final and eternal home with the Father and Son.

We are not alone in our effort to seduce others for Christ. We are empowered by God's Spirit to undertake this very activity.

I spent a year in the early 1970s living in southern England. While there, I met a young woman who graciously invited me to lunch at her home next to the university campus in Southampton. We had met at a conference in London and, as is so often the case with Christians, we felt an immediate bond of faith and fellowship.

During lunch, she asked me a question that startled and unsettled me, "Who have you targeted for Christ?"

"What do you mean?" I asked.

She said matter-of-factly, "Who are you attempting to win to the Lord?"

"Are you sure we're supposed to target people?" I asked hesitantly. It sounded a bit like a fox hunt to me.

She explained, "I believe we are. I believe we are to ask the Holy Spirit who He is bringing our way, and then we are to pray for those people and be very focused in our prayers. We are to look continually for ways to present Christ to them, in the most appealing ways possible. And we are to be available to help them make a commitment of their lives to Christ when they are ready to do so."

Are lost sinners "lawful" targets to be saved? Of course.

Is the conversion of the lost a righteous goal in God's eyes? Absolutely.

Can Christ be presented to lost souls without trickery or deceit? Most definitely.

The questions then remain: What can I do to bring Christ to the attention of a person? What can I do to continually hint that Christ has more to offer a person? What can I do to give persons a memorable gift of Christ's love—making a sacrificial gift to them on Christ's behalf, for Christ's cause, and in the process, meet a need in their life?

Years after this experience in England, I met a couple in the greater Los Angeles area who had the same goal, although they couched it in slightly different terms.

The wife said to me, "We figure that if the Lord brings a couple to our awareness and they don't know Christ, then the Lord intends for us to introduce Him to them and them to Him. So we invite them to dinner. We spare no expense and do everything within our power to make the evening memorable. During dinner, we ask them to share their love story with us. They generally ask us, in return, to tell our story. We tell how we fell in love, and then how we fell in love all over again when we both came to know the Lord Jesus in a personal, intimate way in our lives and marriage."

The couple invited to dinner, of course, invariably feels a need to return the invitation. This gives my friends a second opportunity to share their faith. At this second dinner engagement, they take along a thank you gift. In one instance they gave a couple a special Bible they had purchased in Israel. They underlined certain passages that were meaningful to them—passages that spoke specifically of God's love and care. They suggested the couple read various passages together.

"And then," the wife explained, "we wait for a response. If they ask more questions, we make ourselves available to answer them. If they are ready to make a commitment to Christ, or request prayer, we are available. The outcome of the relationship is up to God. We have done our part, however, in making the introduction."

What might you do today to seduce a person to accept Christ, or to grow further in his or her relationship with Him? How might you bring Christ up in a conversation? Can you find a way to introduce Christ at an important crossroads in the person's life, or during a time of need or trouble? Can you do so in a way that is gracious, honest, and generous?

Be creative! Think seduction!

Some Christians do this by inviting their friends to teas, Bible studies, women's conferences, or seasonal performances and events at their church.

Some do this by giving a person a meaningful spiritual gift.

Some do this by setting a stage within their own homes for meaningful, quiet, and intimate conversation.

Some do this by being present with a person during a period of grief or sickness.

Can you leave the person with the hint that Christ has something more to give? Come up with your own unique and distinctive methods that reflect your personal style.

It may be a pithy statement or a probing question. It may be an invitation. It may be verbal or written. It may be linked to a special event or come as a surprise to the person.

Who can you legitimately and righteously seduce into a relationship or a deeper relationship with Christ?

Come on now . . . you *have* this power. You need only to think like a woman and use the power to seduce . . . for Christ's sake!

4

The Power to Subdue

Beauty is compelling. It captures the eye, tugs at the heart, tickles the senses, and delights the soul.

Men are certainly not immune to beauty. Some create it, and others fall victim to it every day. But women seem to have a special power for creating beauty.

In my opinion, beauty is the "subduing" of ugliness.

Ugliness wasn't an original part of God's creation. Repeatedly we find God saying about His work, "It is good." What else, frankly, could God have said about His own handiwork? The very fact that He allowed it to exist implies that it was good. If it hadn't been good, He would not have made it or allowed it to continue.

God's good and perfect creation was handed over to humankind not only for continuation, but also for "controlled expansion." Two times in the book of Genesis God commands humankind to be fruitful, to multiply, to fill the earth, and to have dominion, or control, over the fish, birds, and animals.

The first command is recorded in Genesis 1:28. Very specifically, God gave Adam and Eve dominion over the Garden of Eden.

The second command is recorded in Genesis 9:1–2. God blessed Noah and his sons and told them to repopulate the earth.

Because Noah's wife and daughters-in-law were part of the group that floated in the ark to survival in the new age, we can assume that even if God did not give the command directly to them, they were engaged in the work associated with that command.

Today women are still under that command. No other command has superseded it. Women are to be fruitful, multiply, fill the earth, and have dominion over it. Women are to continue with ardent effort to bring into being a good and perfect natural world.

"But," you may say, "the earth is presently in a fallen state. It's impossible to restore Eden or to bring the earth back into line with its original perfection."

That most certainly is so. And yet, God gave His second command to humankind to be fruitful, multiply, fill the earth, and have dominion *after* the fall of man and woman in the Garden. Indeed, He gave it after the Flood!

Have you ever experienced a flood? I have never had my house flooded, but I have been forced from my home with the threat of a flood—a full evacuation, apart from two heavy bookcases I couldn't move. I've seen the aftermath of a flood. It's far from a pretty sight. In fact, in cases of severe flooding, the aftermath scenes are ones of total devastation and ugliness. The stench is terrible. The mud and murky waters are filled with unsavory forms of life. The debris is unbelievable. Trees and other plant life that have been under water for any length of time look dead, even if they are not, and they usually take months or years to recover.

It was while pointing to an after-flood world that God said to His original boat people, "Go out now and fill this earth with My perfection."

What a task Eve, Mrs. Noah, Mrs. Ham, Mrs. Shem, and Mrs. Japheth faced. I like to think of these women as charter members of the earthwide garden club. God gave them the authority and the ability to accomplish the task. They were responsible for fulfilling at least 50 percent of the commandment.

God doesn't command us to do that which He doesn't think we can do, or that which He doesn't equip us to do.

....

The Elements of Beauty

What is required for something to be termed beautiful? Beauty is certainly an individual evaluation. And yet, we tend to have universal agreement on several points.

Beauty Has Order and Balance

A symmetry of design has beauty. Balanced color tones are beautiful. Form flowing with function creates an object of beauty. We may not be able to describe just why we find something beautiful, but nearly always the thing or person labeled as beautiful has an orderly balance of individual components.

Beauty Must Create an Inner Peace

We all know how our impression of a gorgeous woman or handsome man can be shattered by a raucous or annoying laugh, a grating voice, an obscene gesture, or crude behavior. Beauty appeals to all the senses: sight, hearing, touch, smell, taste.

When something or someone is appealing, we find a great comfort level when we are in the presence of that person, place, or thing. We relax in the beautiful garden. We feel at home and alive as we walk the pristine beach or pause in a field of springtime flowers in the mountain meadow. Even the remembrance of beauty triggers our senses and evokes in us a sense of calm and tranquillity. And what is equally amazing is that scenes of beauty can trigger this calm even if they are photographs or paintings of places we have never experienced in person! Yes, beauty pleases all the senses and in that, brings about a sense of peace.

Beauty Transcends Words

We run out of language trying to describe that which is truly beautiful to us. Tears and smiles and leaps of joy come much closer to being genuine responses to beauty. We gasp or exclaim when we recognize it. Or, we stand in utter awe.

Beauty Evokes Deep Feelings of Meaning

When we encounter genuine beauty, our attention is invariably drawn to the divine and spiritual. Beauty is, in many ways, a metaphor to us for God's very nature. We know that beauty ultimately is His gift to us, and that it is a manifestation of one aspect of His being.

....

Inner Beauty Is True Beauty

Physical beauty doesn't last. The rosebud blooms and withers, the sunset fades, the young woman grows old. What lasts, however, is spiritual beauty—inner beauty that gives a glow to life.

Inner spiritual beauty is more difficult to discern at times, and yet it is true beauty. It brings with it a sense of order, symmetry, purpose, comfort, and physical peace.

One of the most beautiful women I have ever known was deeply wrinkled and frail in body. She was beautiful because of her character and her love.

One of the most beautiful voices I have ever heard belonged to a woman who, by our society's standards, would be deemed physically unattractive. Yet the song and the spiritual quality she conveyed in her singing made this woman a beautiful person.

Indeed, beauty *is* as beauty does. Inner beauty gives rise to outer beauty. It is the spirit that causes beauty to last. True and lasting beauty comes from the inside out.

This is good news! It means that a person who does not have a beautiful body or face can still be a beautiful person.

It means that beauty can exist anywhere on the earth, in any situation, culture, or environment.

It means that beauty is not dependent on youth.

It means that beauty can be achieved and that it can last.

It means that any woman on earth can become beautiful and remain beautiful!

I believe it is this inner beauty that God had in mind when He said to Eve and the women of Noah's family: "Multiply, be fruitful, fill the earth, and have dominion."

To multiply meant far more than the bearing of many children. It meant for these women to multiply their talents, wisdom, and skills among the women who followed them. The intent was for these women to multiply their influence.

To be fruitful meant more than conceiving, or of producing work. The challenge God gave these women was to be a continually bubbling fountain of creativity and productivity.

To fill the earth meant to completely fill the earth. At the point when all the earth is filled with beauty, there will be no room left for any ugliness. We know the application of this in the garden. It isn't enough to pull a weed. We must plant a flower in its place to "fill" the spot of earth. Otherwise, a new weed seed will find a place to take root. To fill the earth means to *fully* reverse a trend toward ugliness.

To have dominion meant to bring back order and balance among the species. This is environmental work—the recreating of a beautiful balance in which humankind, animals, birds, and fish can occupy their respective places and coexist for the benefit of each other. Men and women are in charge of the process. This does not mean that they are to worship animals or exalt them above human beings. Rather, it means that they are to bring about a balance between humankind and beast that has order, symmetry, purpose, and delight as its hallmarks.

The Practical Application of Beauty

How do women make the world a more beautiful place? At least six areas of the world need to be made beautiful.

Women Are Challenged to Beautify Their Time

"Time?" you ask. I can almost see your eyebrows rise. Yes, time.

Few of us think about beautifying our time. Instead, we think about taking time to be beautiful! And yet, the Scriptures tell us very clearly that the beautification of our time is one of the most important projects we can undertake.

Recall these elements of beauty: order, balance, symmetry, harmony, peacefulness, spirituality.

In beautifying our time, we are bringing order, balance, and symmetry to our time. We are managing our time in such a way that we move through our days with a sense of harmony, peace, and rest, as opposed to feeling frantic, in disarray, harried and hassled, pressured, or stressed out. When our time is beautified, we find more meaning in our lives.

We've all heard the phrase, "Take time to smell the roses." That's part of the beautification of time. We need to take time to relax and enjoy the world around us. But if we spend all afternoon smelling the roses, we won't smell the aroma of dinner! We are challenged to find a balance between work and rest, between going and stopping, between taking in and giving out.

Jesus said our priority is to seek the kingdom of God. (See Matt. 6:33.) In a very practical way for many women, this means putting God first in the morning. For some women, it means getting up a half hour or an hour before everyone else in the home and spending that time in prayer, meditation, reading the Scriptures, writing in personal journals, listening to praise music—in other words, spending time talking to and listening to the Lord. For some women, it means sitting down for a "tea time" in the afternoon before children and husband arrive home, and using that time for reflection, relaxation, and reprioritization—again, reading the Scriptures, talking to the Lord, and giving themselves space to think about His kingdom and His purposes for their life on the earth. For some women it means taking the lunch hour at work to close the office door and relax in the Lord's presence, or taking a long walk in a nearby park to reflect on a particular passage of Scripture.

However you choose to carve up the time of your day, you need to find a way in which to "seek first the kingdom of God." Set aside time and space so that God can get a word in edgewise. This time and space needs to be an inviolable part of your schedule. *You have the power to make it happen!*

Another key aspect of beautifying time is to give yourself time to do each task in your day well. For most women, this probably means eliminating a good number of tasks.

Our culture tells us, "You can have it all and do it all." I add to that, "But not all at the same time." The more tasks, responsibilities, and relationships we cram into twenty-four hours a day, the less time we have for each one of them, and the more pressure we feel about all of them. Do what you do well, in a timely manner, and with sufficient time allotted. In so doing, you'll feel better and your day will take on a glow that can be described only as beautiful.

Another way to beautify time is to flow with time rather than fight against it.

I have a tendency to schedule myself very tightly. As a result, I often race against deadlines, feel frantic in my effort not to be late, and in the breakneck speed, I make mistakes, which serve only to slow me down and add more pressure!

I'm working to correct this tendency in a concerted way these days, and as I take each small step toward a looser schedule, I'm finding that life is becoming more beautiful. The difference is often one of perspective, of saying "I hope to" rather than "I must" about any particular activity or event on the calendar.

The practical change is that I am scheduling downtime and refusing to schedule work during certain hours or on certain specified days. I'm making an effort to keep the Sabbath day holy and *wholly* unto the purpose God intended. I'm refusing to work after a certain hour of the day and after lunch on Saturdays.

These changes in perspective and schedule allow room for the unexpected to happen—and, of course, it invariably does. One thing I'm discovering, however, is that the unexpected is *good* at least half of the time. In opening up my schedule, I have a feeling that I just may be allowing the Lord an opportunity to send blessings!

Women Are Challenged to Beautify Their Activities

Even as we beautify our time, we are to beautify what we do.

When we give ourselves an ordered and yet relaxed schedule, we are more capable of giving more time and attention to everything we undertake. We have a few extra moments to arrange the flowers we bought at the market, rather than plunk them down haphazardly in any nearby vase. We have a few extra minutes to arrange a garnish for the dish, or to light the candles on the dining table. We have the extra ninety seconds that it takes to wrap the gift and tie a ribbon around it, rather than hand it to a friend unceremoniously.

In beautifying our activities, we give them meaning. Perhaps at no time and in no way is this more important than during celebrations. It's not enough that we free up our schedules to give ourselves time to celebrate. We must put true and meaningful celebration into the time we've set aside. Generally speaking, this means infusing symbolism into what we do, or taking the extra effort to add more order or meaning to what we do.

As you seek out gifts to give on special days of celebration, ask yourself: What is the most meaningful gift I can give right now? Convey to the person to whom you give a gift what it meant for you to purchase the item and what you hope the item will mean to the other person.

As you plan meals, keep the people who will be at the dinner table in mind. What do they enjoy eating? What extra effort can you put into the meal to make it truly a balanced, ordered, lovely, beautiful event?

As you think of activities that surround a celebration—whether decorating the Christmas tree, singing "Happy Birthday," or baking a cake—think of ways in which you can add even more beauty to the event. Are all the senses being triggered in a wonderful way? Will the atmosphere be one that invites each person into the celebration, or makes each person feel comfortable? What more can you do to give meaning to the activity? Have you allowed for quiet moments of awe?

Study the feast days of the Old Testament, which were festivals that Jesus and His disciples and the members of the early church kept faithfully, to see how God plans a celebration. Every detail is ordered. Every physical sense is triggered. Meaning infuses all activities. These are called days of rest, in which no work is to be done. They were high, holy days—high referring to their priority before God and man, and holy referring to the fact that they were separate from the normal way of the world.

Do you have any high, holy days in your year? What do you do during them? What more can you do to make them a top priority, an expression of worship, days that are unlike any other day?

You have what it takes to beautify your celebrations and to create special moments and special memories!

Women Are Challenged to Beautify Their Own Lives

A number of Bible women are described as being beautiful: Sarah, Rebekah, Rachel, Abigail, Esther, Job's daughters, and Tamar. It's easy to assume that these women had a natural beauty and grace.

Consider, however, how difficult it was in Bible times for even a "natural beauty" to remain beautiful. The desert climate of the Middle East, often marked by extreme heat, wind, and very dry conditions, was brutal on skin and hair. Fresh, clean water was not readily available in all times and at all places. Travel was by foot for the most part, and many women worked very hard, making it difficult for a woman to have beautiful hands and feet.

The point is . . . even beautiful women in the Bible had to work at staying that way. How much more so those who weren't naturally beautiful!

The Bible has numerous references to jewels, ornaments, and accessories. Bible women used perfumes, ointments, bath oils, and sachets. They bathed often and ritually washed their hands before meals and their feet upon entering homes.

Bible women were just as concerned about their appearance as women today. We need to recognize that Bible women did not have all of the modern conveniences we have today. Bible women worked hard physically. They did not sit idly in the boudoir before a lighted mirror.

True beauty, however, is marked by a sense of inner order, balance, and meaning.

Of all the many wonderful attributes given about the virtuous woman in Proverbs 31, only one reference is made to her appearance and it is this: "She makes tapestry for herself; her clothing is fine linen and purple" (v. 22).

On the other hand, the description of the virtuous woman ends this way: "Charm is deceitful and beauty is passing, but a woman who fears the LORD, she shall be praised. Give her of the fruit of her hands, and let her own works praise her in the gates" (vv. 30–31).

What can we conclude about this in applying the balance of the Bible to our own lives? We are to make the most with what we have given our physical attributes, weight, economic conditions, level of health, and all other factors. And then we are to get busy. At all times we are to "fear the Lord," following His commandments and living according to His principles. It is our obedience to the Lord, our inner spirituality, that will bring us praise. It is our work that brings us reward.

Dress well. Be clean. Fix your hair in a becoming style. Wear cosmetics and perfume if you want. But don't make any of these things your be-all and end-all of life. Remember that the keys to beauty are balance, order, symmetry, harmony, and a delight for all senses.

You may need to work on your manners, or on the quality and tenor of your voice. You may need to bring more order to your wardrobe, or work on improving your health. All of these are aspects of beauty.

But, work on your inner spirituality above all. Seek to become more and more like Jesus in your character and motivations. Study His Word. Talk to Him daily. Focus on the things that are important to Him. And do what He asks you to do. Let your beauty shine from the inside out.

My mother used to tell me, "Having fine animals and good quality hay inside the barn is what gives the barn its true value. But an occasional new coat of red paint on the barn doesn't hurt." I still find that to be excellent advice.

Women Are Challenged to Beautify Their Families

We are to encourage our family members to be just as beautiful as we ourselves desire to be—both inside and outside.

What are you teaching your daughter or son about beauty? (Yes, boys need to be taught how to beautify themselves, too!) How are you helping your daughter to order her life, make her walk with the Lord her first priority, have a balanced perspective on her appearance, gain fine manners and poise? How are you helping your son to see that he is more than his body, and that his reputation ultimately will flow from spiritual attributes, not physical ones or career successes? How are you helping your husband to be a more beautiful person?

This is not a throwback to the 1960s when we all could sing the song, "Everybody's beautiful, in their own way." The beautiful-people concept of the 1960s had a very definite look. The so-called beautiful women of that time were unconventional. They tended to shun makeup and wear beads, sandals, and tie-dyed clothing. Whereas the emphasis was placed theoretically on the beauty of the person's inner life, in actuality, beauty was marked by a person's willingness to rebel against society and experiment with new ideas and new drugs. Twenty years later, beautiful people were those considered to be living the lifestyles of the rich and famous. Fashion is fickle. It isn't true beauty.

Being a truly beautiful person means that your life has order and purpose to it, both of which flow from your spiritual life. Being a beautiful person means that you attempt to call more attention to Christ than you do to yourself.

And what about your parents? You may not have considered helping your parents stay beautiful as they age, and yet they are an extension of you. What can you do to help your parents have a deeper spiritual life, a more ordered material world, a cleaner environment, a more lovely appearance?

A friend of mine routinely took her mother with her to the beauty parlor, and gave her mother gifts of facials and nail care—even when my friend was sixty-five and her mother was eighty-eight. I had an opportunity to visit the mother just a few days before her death. She knew she was dying, and her voice was very weak. Even so, her hair was freshly brushed, and her nails had been trimmed and brightly polished just the day before! The light in her eyes was the truly beautiful part of her appearance, however. The reflected glow of heaven radiated from them.

Women Are Challenged to Beautify Their Homes

Most women delight in decorating their homes and don't consider it to be the least bit of a chore. To beautify a home, however, means to do more than clean it and make it pretty.

Beautification also means to bring order and comfort to a dwelling. In bringing order, you should have necessary items accessible for use, clean when needed, and fully repaired for use. To bring order means to sort, which in turn means to get rid of what you don't need or can't use. Some of your leftovers are best given to others or recycled back into the manufacturing process. Other items are best trashed.

In bringing comfort to a home, you need to take into consideration the needs and personality of each family member. A home has little value if it is only a showcase place for visitors. Rather, a home has value if it is an inviting, fully functional, and relaxing place to those who live within it.

Do you like your furniture? Are you continually worried about something being marred or dirtied? Have you made the atmosphere warm and cozy with sunlight, candles, good books, living plants or flowers, pliable cushions, and other objects that help turn a house into a home?

Is there a space that everybody in your home can call exclusively his or her own? It might be only a bed or a chair. For a home to be a beautiful place, a person needs to feel it is his or her place.

Do you have a schedule for keeping your home and the things in it repaired, cleaned, and maintained?

Do other people feel welcome in your home? Do you know how to be a genuinely generous hostess?

The Scriptures have numerous references about our willingness to share our homes with fellow believers. Many homes in Old Testament days had "prophet's chambers" in which righteous travelers were invited to stay. The early Christians met in homes for their worship services.

Your home is to be the primary place of Christian service in your life. It is when you make it a place of spiritual refuge and spiritual service that it truly becomes beautiful.

Women Are Challenged to Beautify the Earth

For most women, this means a responsibility to beautify the parcel of earth over which they have direct control.

I had no difficulty with this when I lived in a high-rise apartment. I beautified my balcony with a couple of big pots of geraniums! Now, however, I have a yard to mow, bushes to trim, leaves to rake, and bulbs to plant. I don't have dominion yet, but I'm gaining on it. There's much more beauty and order and purpose to this plot of ground than there was twelve years ago when the soil was sandy, weedy, and covered with anthills.

I am inspired by the older couple who live across the street. They have a large vegetable garden, a perfectly manicured lawn, healthy trees, and an abundance of flowers. They've managed their particular plot very well, and they have even taken dominion over the vacant lot next door to them, having purchased it, sodded it, and planted flowers on it. They are far better gardeners than I, but I'm learning!

In a very minor but important way, I am responsible for pollution control, drainage engineering, procreation of species, pollination, soil enrichment, and animal refuge in my little corner of the world. My garden is *my* responsibility and no one else's. It's my primary contribution to the total ecology and beautification of the earth.

If each person on the earth took on the beautification of just one acre of ground, what a world we would live in! But every person doesn't have an acre under his or her control. Some have many thousands of acres. Some have none. And some acres have nobody in charge. As a result, we each have responsibility for doing what we can to beautify the whole—to be concerned about the care of the whole earth.

Wherever you have ability and authority, you are to ask the Lord what action He desires for you to take. It may be active involvement related to particular species or regions of the world.

It may be making choices *not* to use resources in excess. It may involve work of other kinds: writing letters, sending checks, leading discussions.

Again, the goal is not only appearance, but order, balance, and meaning.

Everyone knows what it means to be inspired by nature. Some people are very much at home tramping through the woods to hike, photograph, or hunt . . . or wading into rivers to fish or swim . . . or slushing down slopes for the thrill of the speed and fresh air. How many people do you know who say that they feel closer to God in nature?

As a Christian, whatever you do with regard to the natural world as a whole must be couched in terms of a spiritual goal. You must ask yourself, "How can others feel more of God's presence in this place?" The answers will differ depending on where you are standing at the time you ask the question. If you're standing in a dump site, you'll have one answer. If you're standing in a clearing in the High Sierra, you'll have another. If you're standing on a beach, you'll have still another answer.

There's no one universal "Christian" response to the environment, other than the fact that humans are to have dominion over the species—to care for them, keep them in balance, and use them in ways God has designated. When we have done that, we will have created a world that has greater meaning for both humankind and the creatures of the field, sky, and sea.

Adding Beauty to the Kingdom of God

When you think of beauty and the kingdom of God, do you think only of great cathedrals, memorial gardens, stained glass windows, and celestial music?

Churches *should* be beautiful places of worship, and more such places should be created. There's no excuse for ugly buildings or furnishings in places designated for holy worship to the Lord God Almighty. Part of the function of a church is beauty!

Recall again the characteristics of beauty: order, balance, symmetry, harmony, peacefulness, and spirituality.

The kingdom of God as a whole needs to bear these qualities. When we as a Church, not merely our church buildings, have these qualities, we will attract others to us in droves. The comfort and meaning and beauty that we offer to a world filled with ugliness (both in behavior and appearance) will be utterly compelling!

For us to beautify the kingdom of God, we must recognize first that we have the authority and ability to do this as women. Beautifying the kingdom means more than making sure the candles are trimmed and a beautiful floral bouquet is in place before the altar or pulpit. Beautifying the kingdom means more than making sure that the organ is in tune and the choir is fully gathered.

Beautifying the kingdom means we . . .

Insist on Peace Within the Church

Wherever we see conflict, we speak out for resolution. Wherever we see alienation, we do what we can to bring about reconciliation. Wherever we see extraneous and purposeless noise, we request immediate silence. Wherever the silence is filled with hatred and distrust, we request immediate communication.

Jesus said, "Blessed are the peacemakers." And He added that they become the sons (and daughters) of God. (See Matt. 5:9.) As followers of Christ, we must insist that we all come to a place of unity within the body of Christ. Only then can we truly have order, purpose, and an attractiveness to win souls to Him.

This unity must never be a false state, but a genuine one. We must talk and pray and work together until we agree on who we are in Christ, and who He is in us.

This does not mean that we lose our diversity of culture,

race, or gender, or that we invalidate any particular opinion. It does mean that we come together as one and decide which direction to move as a body, and how we will operate in reaching out to those in need.

In our board meetings and committee meetings within the Church we need to have unanimous votes. Feelings of dissent don't evaporate after a democratic majority-rule vote. (A democratic majority-win vote is the norm of the American political system. There's no place in God's Word where majority rule is in place.) The 49 percent who vote against something are likely to remain the 49 percent who oppose something. This kind of dissent festers, brews, seethes, and ultimately erupts and divides. We work, talk, pray, and pray some more until we have something on which we can all agree is in God's plan and purpose for His Church, and to which we all can commit our time and effort wholeheartedly.

Jesus said that He and the Father are One. The writers of the epistles called the Church to be one in the Spirit. Paul wrote that we in the Church are to acknowledge one body, one Spirit, one hope, one Lord, one faith, one baptism, one God and Father of all "who is above all, and through all, and in you all." (See Eph. 4:1–6.)

Insist on Order Within the Church

Paul taught that the Spirit brought order to the Church, and that all things were to be conducted in an orderly fashion. This does not mean that we need to legislate, organize, or politicize the church into hierarchies and rules that stifle the flow of God's presence and power within our church bodies. God forbid!

It does mean that our service to God—our worship—must be done in a way that the Spirit directs and orders.

The Spirit does not direct believers to compete, in either word or deed, or for segments of a budget. The Spirit challenges believers to cooperate "with all lowliness and gentleness, with longsuffering, bearing with one another in love" (Eph. 4:2).

The Spirit does not direct believers to become cliquish. All are to be one body. As a Christian woman, you can take a very personal and private stand for true spiritual orderliness by refusing to belong to or participate in any club, group, or class that closes its door to other believers—for any reason.

Refuse to compete. If someone suggests a campaign that pits one side of the church against another, or even a campaign that pits your church against another church in your city, refuse to participate. Voice your concern.

Insist on Total Appeal

The beauty of your church, and the beauty of the believers with whom you worship, should be appealing to visitors. What do you give to visitors who come in your door? Do you have a special gift of beauty awaiting them?

Will your gift of beauty trigger all of their senses with delight? Will they see beauty . . . hear beauty . . . taste beauty . . . smell beauty . . . touch beauty? Will they understand the meaning of what you do? Will they feel at home, at peace, at rest in your presence? Will they respond to what you do with emotions that run deeper than words?

You have the ability to give visitors to your church an experience of genuine beauty, one that will stand in sharp contrast to the ugliness they may be experiencing in their own lives or in the world outside your door.

If you were hosting a dinner party for the president of the United States, or any other person you deem to be very important, you no doubt would use your best china and silverware, have flowers on the table, fix the most delectable meal, and do your utmost to make the person feel at home. You'd probably have something special planned for the person—perhaps music, a gift of some kind, or a unique experience.

Friends of mine were hosts to a British lord at their ranch. They used their finest service for the meal they served him. They took him to see their longhorn cattle and the few head of buffalo they kept. They gave him a gift unique to the old West. They served him the biggest steak he had ever seen. And in the end he said, "I have only one question for you. Can I come back?"

Who is about to come to your church or into your circle of believing friends for the first time? Will she want to come back?

Insist on Spiritual Meaning

Finally, insist on spiritual meaning of the highest order. All that you do should be pointed toward the Lord, not yourself. He is the King of Glory.

How do you do this in a practical way? In the same ways you spiritually undergird all of your personal and practical beautification efforts. You place most of your time in any one gathering upon the Lord—upon hearing His Word, praying to Him, doing that which is pleasing to Him. You truly praise and worship Him.

This sounds obvious, and yet how many meetings or services have you attended under the broad umbrella of the church in which most of the time was spent talking about human problems, business topics, legislative issues, or upcoming events? You must beautify your time when you are gathered in the name of the Lord.

You must reinfuse meaning into your activities. Many people no longer know or remember the meaning of the symbols and actions associated with the rituals of the Church. And every church and every denomination have their own unique set of rituals. You must remember the Christian services and rituals and remind yourself of what it is that Christ did that compelled the Church to respond in these ritualistic ways.

At the same time, there's certainly opportunity to create new traditions and celebrations. You can draw from Scripture and church history and your own miracle moments, and then celebrate the remembrance of these events in the most meaningful ways possible.

Christians must adorn themselves as "bodies" of believers. Are there those in your midst who need a practical, loving touch of beauty in their lives, or who need help in a particular area of adornment? What evening meeting or retreat weekend might you create to invite women to engage in greater personal beautification, both spiritual and physical? Perhaps you can invite women to explore the topic of beauty as it is portrayed in the Bible, or give women an opportunity to share their beauty secrets. Keep the emphasis on inner beauty first, outer beauty second.

You can plan similar experiences for children and for men. What does it mean to be a truly beautiful teenager, child, man of God?

Christians must beautify the houses of worship. Is there something in your place of worship that can be upgraded for greater beauty? Can you make your church more beautiful with new candles, cushions, or rugs?

A church in my city recently repaired and remodeled its interior and as part of the process, the women of the church stitched dozens of beautiful needlepoint kneeling cushions. Each cushion was filled with symbolism. What a beautiful expression of spiritual life!

Does everything within your church have spiritual meaning? It can.

Does every aspect of your worship service focus on the Lord and draw attention to His holiness, majesty, and love? It can.

And what about the grounds surrounding your church? Are they a delight?

Is your witness in the community marked by beauty? Do you have well-ordered, meaningful outreach programs to your community? Do community members feel comfortable when members of your group call on them or when they participate in your church's events?

Women have the authority and the ability to infuse beauty into *all* that they do, in both their personal lives and the kingdom of God. They have the power to multiply their influence, sharing with an ever-widening circle of women the "beauty tricks" that work for them. They have the power to be exceedingly fruitful, creating new objects, programs, conferences, and messages that inspire others to add beauty to every aspect of their lives. They have the power to fill the earth with beauty, to restore their homes and gardens and very lives to a position of order, harmony, pleasure, and peace. They have the power to take dominion over the creatures of the earth, and bring about a balance between humankind and nature that is healthful, helpful, and inspiring.

As a Christian woman you have the power to subdue the disarray, disharmony, and dissonance of our world!

You have what it takes!

5

··

The
Power to
Transact

Women have the power to conduct transactions, including the power to transact business.

Business covers a wide range of activities, including manufacturing, budgeting, buying and selling, saving and investing, bartering and trading, marketing and advertising. Many women who don't think of themselves as businesswomen will readily admit that they are fabulous shoppers. Well, shopping is business. It is a type of transaction!

I know of no one who is better at shopping than my friend Bobi, especially when it comes to shopping in foreign markets. When Bobi and I strolled through a commercial district in Jerusalem, I learned that shopping is a form of recreation for Bobi. She delights in finding the best quality, and then in negotiating the lowest price, all the while winning the respect of the seller. She truly knows how to get the most for the least amount of money.

She lives within driving distance of some of the greatest wholesale markets in the world. She thinks nothing of being at the flower market at 5:30 A.M. to purchase $500 worth of flowers, which she and other volunteers will transform by means of thirty hours of labor into a floral extravaganza for a friend's wedding—

a "gift" that would otherwise have cost upward of $5,000. She knows where to get remnants of the best quality fabrics, which she then turns into exotic shawls, pillows, and window treatments.

When someone asked her to secure an outdoor site for an international conference, she delighted in sitting down over Turkish coffee and slowly and methodically negotiating the contract with the Arab landowners.

Bobi knows how to shop and how to make transactions. And in my experience, I have found that most women do.

Women read labels, look for bargains, and know when a sale is really a good one. Women find deals. They know how to put together a garage sale and turn the proceeds into new furniture. They know how to grow gardens and trade produce with their neighbors. They know how to pool their talents and time and paint the church, make the quilt, or pull off the chili dinner.

Women know how to get the work done and divide their skills, time, and resources to accomplish a task. Yes, women have the power to transact. This power, however, is often expressed in ways that men don't understand.

Imagine a large pile of dirty laundry on a corporate conference table. Around the pile stand a group of men. What is likely to be the conversation?

From my fifteen years of experience in the corporate world, I imagine comments such as these being made:

Well, whose laundry is this?

How did it get here?

Who is responsible for dealing with it?

Is there a message being sent here?

When is this going to be taken care of?

How much is it going to cost to take care of this dirty laundry?

Who can give us an estimate?

Well, it's not coming out of my budget.

Who is going to pay for it?

We need a plan for dealing with this and for similar situations that might arise.

We need to make sure this never happens again, especially on a Monday morning.

And so on. The laundry remains, probably until one of the men finally concludes that it's time for lunch, and he says, "Hey . . . let's go eat. Have your secretary call my secretary and figure out how to get this laundry out of here by the time we get back."

Imagine the same pile of laundry on a table at a family reunion. This time a group of women are standing around it. I imagine them making such comments as these:

Wow! We certainly have a lot of laundry to do.

I'll put the whites in bleach.

I'll start a load of colored clothes.

I'll do the hand laundry.

I'll keep the washing machine going if you'll hang the damp clothes out to dry.

I'll run to the corner store and get some more detergent and fabric softener.

Don't forget to get some stain remover, too. Here's a five-dollar bill to help with the cost.

You fold and I'll put them away.

I'll set up the iron.

And by noon, not only has the laundry been done, but the women have had a great time talking and joking about each of their family members and the woes in their relationships, their neighbors and friends and their woes, and their best new recipes and worst clean-up jobs of the past month.

Has doing the laundry been a transaction? Yes! Time, talent, and resources have been pooled, delegated, and put to use . . . with the end result being the accomplishment of a task. Decisions have been made. A problem has been solved. Power—usually called manpower, but in this case, womanpower—has been exerted to accomplish a goal. And along the way, morale has been maintained.

Transactions, as this example illustrates, cover more than the buying and selling activity of business. Transactions include forging compromises and making treaties, mediating disputes, making decisions, engaging in problem solving, delegating responsibility, pulling together specialized teams to accomplish specific tasks, scheduling deliveries, and creating timetables for work.

The power to transact plays a big role in motherhood! Virtually every mother has had to forge compromises among her children, resolve disputes and settle fights, make on-the-spot decisions, help solve problems, assign chores, make family schedules and calendars, plan future events, and coordinate efforts to get tasks accomplished. These abilities are very real aspects of the power to transact.

One of my friends who sells real estate defines the word *transaction* this way: moving things from the "in" basket to the "out" basket, so that between the times that the sign is flipped from "open" to "closed" the greatest number of "sold" signs can be affixed to "for sale" signs. These principles apply to all types of work.

Women have the ability to do work, to accomplish tasks, and to do so with great efficiency, effectiveness, and quality. Part of getting the job done well is to know the keys to a successful transaction.

Keys to a Successful Transaction

Several Bible women give us important keys as to how women can conduct successful transactions. One of these women is an unnamed widow, whose story is told in 2 Kings 4.

This particular woman's husband died, leaving her with a mountain of debt and two sons. She received word that the creditors were coming to take her sons as slaves in order to resolve the debt, and she immediately went to the prophet Elisha for help.

Elisha asked the widow what she had in her house that was of any value or which might be sold. She replied that the only thing she had that anyone else might want to buy was a jar of oil. She didn't have a lot!

Elisha advised her to borrow as many vessels as she could from all her neighbors, and then to shut herself up in her home with her sons and begin to pour her jar of oil into the vessels. As each vessel became full, she was to set it aside and move on to the next container.

As long as an empty vessel remained in the house, the miraculous flow of oil from her jar continued. When no more empty vessels remained, the oil ceased to flow.

At that point she went back to Elisha, and he told her, "Go, sell the oil and pay your debt; and you and your sons live on the rest" (2 Kings 4:1–7).

There are five aspects of this woman's character that made her transactions a success. Consider these characteristics and how they apply to women today.

Don't Give Up in a Crisis

The widow didn't meekly hand over her sons to the creditors. She didn't wring her hands in silent agony. She scrambled into action. She engaged in the transaction process.

There's nothing in the Scriptures that commands a woman to sit idly by and watch her children be destroyed, misused, or abused. There's nothing in the Scriptures that says a woman should cast herself upon public sympathy when times get tough. Women have an ability to take action when faced with the crisis of debt, or any family crisis, for that matter.

Remember, too, that this woman is in mourning over the

death of her husband. She's going through what most people would consider to be a period of weakness and inner pain. However, she doesn't use her loss as an excuse for not attending to the present realities of her life. This woman has an inner power that compels her to action, even in grief.

Consult an Expert for Advice

A woman does well to seek advice from experts in the field where she needs help. Often these are the people at the top of a company or an organization.

In her particular situation, the widow wasn't afraid to seek advice from the president of the seminary where her husband studied and worked.

Much concern is registered in our society about glass ceilings, and about women not being able to get to the top in the companies where they work. Part of women's inability to get to the top, in my opinion, is that many women are afraid to talk to the people at the top.

These same women, however, would probably have no difficulty marching into the superintendent's office or principal's office at their child's school, in writing a letter to the president of the United States, or in calling the vice-president of sales and service when the product they ordered arrives damaged or isn't repaired properly.

Women, for the most part and in most circumstances, have an intuitive understanding that if they really want to get something in their lives fixed, they need to get the best help possible. And that could mean going all the way to the top for advice or assistance.

Going to the top is a technique of power. To get power, you must align with power. And the most power is at the top of any organization. The widow knew that . . . and that's just where she went.

Have a Proper Understanding of Value

Women have the ability to take stock of their lives—their talents and resources—and to determine what has value in the marketplace.

Two women I know had a food processing business for a few years. They took stock of what they had of value—fruit trees in their backyards, art talent to make a label, access to a commercial kitchen, excellent recipes handed down from their grandmothers, and a community co-op as a sales outlet. They used their free Saturdays for canning, and they used the proceeds from their venture to pay for their children's school clothes.

Another woman I know needed extra money. When she took stock of her resources, she had only a house and a fenced-in yard with some play equipment that had been used by her own five children. Rather than seek a job outside her home, which would have entailed finding day care and after-school care for her own children, she opened her own after-school child care facility.

Women intuitively know what has value and what other women want and are willing to pay for. The widow in the story had only a jar of oil, but she knew it had value.

Don't Be Too Proud to Borrow Or Ask for Help

The widow had the inner courage to borrow from her neighbors. She wasn't seeking a free lunch. She was not being manipulative. She was asking and borrowing. There's a great likelihood that she sold her supply of oil back to the very neighbors from whom she had borrowed containers. In the process, she also asked her sons to assist her in the oil-manufacturing business within her home.

In my experience, women are much better at asking for things than men are. Women aren't afraid to ask for help, ask for directions, ask for details, or ask for suggestions.

Asking is a manifestation of inner power and courage. It is a technique that yields the information and assistance that, in turn, can become an expression of power.

Don't Be Afraid to Take Charge

The widow gathered vessels. She poured oil. She sold oil. She paid her bills. In today's terms, she became a single parent and a sole provider.

What we aren't told directly in this story, but which certainly must have happened, is that this woman had an accounting of her debt. She knew how much she owed in relationship to what she had. She knew what the creditors were exacting. Otherwise, she never would have known when her debt was paid. In other words, this woman was very likely the family bookkeeper.

A number of years ago, I had several conversations with young Christian women who were about to be married. These women had read books or heard speakers advising that a man should be in charge of a family's checkbook, and that it was a husband's responsibility to manage the finances of the family. Some of these women were very skilled in the management of money, both in their personal lives and as part of their corporate jobs.

Each woman told me during our first conversation that she was going to turn over her paychecks to her husband, along with her checkbook and investment portfolio as soon as she returned from the honeymoon. Each woman truly felt it was her Christian duty, and each expressed relief at the prospect.

These women told me during our second conversation—weeks or months after the honeymoon—that they had reassumed not only full responsibility for their own finances, but had assumed responsibility for management of the family budget, including balancing the checkbook and making investments. In some cases, the men they married didn't want the responsibility. In other cases, the men weren't savvy about money. In still other cases, the men didn't feel they had the time for these details.

And in one case, the man had mismanaged the woman into deep debt within a matter of days after their wedding.

Nothing of a spiritual nature was at stake here. The spiritual lives of all these women and their husbands remained strong. Money management, investment management, and property management are practical, material concerns, and women have just as much ability to handle these concerns as men. In our society, they also have just as much authority.

Women also have authority from a scriptural standpoint. There's no place in the Bible where women are admonished to leave all money management or transactions to men. In fact, the "ideal woman" described in Proverbs 31 is portrayed as a woman with a great deal of power to engage in transactions:

The Scriptures say . . .	As we might say . . .
"She seeks wool and flax. . . . She brings her food from afar" (vv. 13–14).	She shops and makes purchases.
"She considers a field and buys it; from her profits she plants a vineyard" (v. 16).	She invests and reinvests.
"She perceives that her merchandise is good" (v. 18).	She knows value and quality.
"She makes linen garments and sells them, and supplies sashes for the merchants" (v. 24).	She manufactures and markets . . . she runs her own business.
"She watches over the ways of her household, and does not eat the bread of idleness" (v. 27).	She knows what is going on in her home. She works!

Frankly, the historical evidence seems to lie on the side of women handling practical day-to-day transactions. Throughout the centuries, women have tended to be the ones to manage family finances. As men went off to hunt game, off to war, off to sea, off to work, women were left to make ends meet at home. In Bible times, women were given dowries, which were always legally theirs. The woman in Jesus' parable who is frantically sweeping her house in search of a lost coin is very likely looking for a missing coin from her dowry headdress. She's lost a piece of her personal wealth and she is determined to find it! (See Luke 15:8–10.)

In our family, my mother kept the books for both the family business and the personal family finances. She paid the bills, managed the checkbook, and routinely discussed investments and major purchases with my father. Most of her friends did the same. Most of the married women I know today also are the managers of the family funds.

The women of my grandmother's era, on the other hand, tended not to take nearly as much interest in the family finances. My grandmother had a home allowance, which she managed masterfully. At my grandfather's death, however, she knew very little about his estate or her future. She faced a major learning curve in knowing how to conduct certain legal and financial transactions.

Both my mother and my grandmother had excellent marriages, secure lives, and the ability to manage funds. My mother need not have managed the family finances, and my grandmother could have managed them if she had wanted to. Nothing spiritual or universal was involved. They simply chose to exercise their power to conduct transactions in different ways.

Actually, although my grandmother didn't handle family finances, she did make a great many real estate investments through the years, and she did find innovative ways of providing shelter and financial security for her own mother and several other relatives. Plus, she knew how to spend very efficiently the money my grandfather gave her, always managing to have funds put away for special things she wanted to own or do.

The point is women can take charge of business if they choose to do so. The power to transact is theirs to use as they will, or as they need. The widow in the Bible story illustrates that point. At no time does Elisha tell her to leave the matter to him or to other men. At no time does he reprimand her for her take-charge attitude or behavior.

····························

Abigail's Important Transaction with David

One of the Bible women who best exemplifies a woman's power to conduct transactions is Abigail.

Abigail is described in the Bible as "a woman of good understanding and beautiful appearance" (1 Sam. 25:3). In other words, she had both brains and beauty. She was married to a difficult man, Nabal, who is described as "harsh and evil in his doings."

David protected Nabal's shepherds as they grazed their flocks near Carmel. As the story is told in the Bible, the time for sheep shearing had come, which was always a festive time in the spring with much feasting. David sent ten of his men to Nabal's house with a request that Nabal send food back to David's camp as a reward for the help David's soldiers had provided. David's request was neither abnormal nor presumptuous. He knew Nabal had prepared feasts for the shearers and that he was very capable of sending the gift David had requested. This request was more akin to a polite request for payment due.

Nabal responded, in essence, by saying to David's men, "I don't know David, so why should I believe his story or provide for him and his men? For all I know, you men are renegades."

The men returned to David with this insulting message and David, in turn, marshalled four hundred of his six-hundred-member army and prepared to pay a visit to Nabal.

Meanwhile, one of the young men in Nabal's household reported to Abigail what had happened, and what was happening. This young man said to Abigail, "Consider what you will do, for harm is determined against our master and against all his household. For he is such a scoundrel that one cannot speak to him" (1 Sam. 25:17).

Abigail hurriedly put together a generous gift of food—two hundred loaves of bread, two skins of wine, five dressed sheep, about eleven thousand bushels of roasted grain, a hundred clusters of raisins, and two hundred fig cakes. The very fact that Abigail was able to put together such a vast amount of food tells us how wealthy Nabal was, and how much food was readily available.

Abigail had the food loaded onto donkeys and sent her servants to David, and then she followed the entourage on her own donkey. She told nothing of this to Nabal.

When Abigail got near David's camp, David and his men came out to meet her and told her what they had planned for Nabal and all the men of his household. Abigail fell on her face before David, and she made a fairly long plea to him. She said as part of her plea, "Let this iniquity be on me. Please let me speak with you. My husband may have said what he said, but I did not see your young men. Since you haven't engaged in this bloodshed yet, please reconsider. Accept my offering of food on Nabal's behalf, and enjoy the Lord's blessing rather than take revenge that might bring God's displeasure on your life."

Throughout her plea to David, Abigail repeatedly praised his character, expressed her belief in his position before the Lord, and requested his favor. She provided an "out" for David to change his mind and still be perceived as a noble leader by his men. Her words provide a masterful study in effective communication!

David calmed down, thanked Abigail, accepted her gift of food, and said to her, "Blessed is your advice and blessed are you. . . . Go up in peace to your house. See, I have heeded your voice and respected your person" (1 Sam. 25:33, 35).

Abigail returned home and found Nabal eating a feast befitting a king. He was drunk, so Abigail wisely said nothing to him. The next morning, however, when Nabal was sober, she told him what nearly happened and what she had done. The shock of the news caused Nabal to have a stroke (or perhaps a heart attack). Ten days later, he died.

When David heard of Nabal's death, he proposed to Abigail and she became his wife.

Abigail went from being the wife of a man who thought himself a king, to being the wife of a man who was truly destined to be a king.

What a transaction Abigail conducted! She did so without consulting her husband and without seeking his input. This does not mean that she was not submissive, or that she was acting beyond her authority as a wife. Submission has nothing to do with this story. Rather, Abigail exercised her full authority and privilege as Nabal's wife. She made a basic assumption that she had just as much to lose as Nabal did should David and his men descend in fury upon their home, and she accurately assessed the situation: If she didn't act, she wouldn't have a husband or a home!

Granted, Abigail was facing a crisis. At another time, she may not have acted without telling Nabal what she was doing. Nonetheless, Abigail had courage to face this critical moment, make a wise decision, and carry out her plan of action quickly and completely. She didn't cower in face of the challenge. She believed within herself that she had the power, both the ability and authority, to make this transaction, and she took action.

The biblical principle related to a woman's power to transact is this: *A woman always has the authority to take action that is for good, and which is for the preservation of her life, the lives of her loved ones, and her home.*

Furthermore, Abigail engaged in the transaction process personally. She didn't hide behind paperwork, emissaries, or servants. She met David on his turf and addressed him directly, fully following the protocol of the day so that her words might be couched in the graciousness of refined manners.

Abigail stated her case plainly, forcefully, and courageously. She didn't mince words. Everything about her life was on the line at that point, and she spoke boldly to the one man who held the key to changing the tide that was rising against her and her family.

Abigail's example tells us this: *A woman has the power to speak her mind—even when speaking to the most powerful man in the land, on his turf, and before his associates.*

Abigail was generous. She gave David more than he had requested or expected. She illustrates this: *A woman is more effective in conducting transactions when she is generous in spirit.*

And finally, Abigail didn't withhold information from her husband. Rather, she reported to him what she had done and why, at a time when he was able to hear her. She didn't confront him when he was drunk. She didn't attempt to be rational when he was irrational. She chose her timing carefully.

Women are wise in their transactions when they

- zero in on what is necessary and important, and concentrate on that;
- make sound decisions in a timely manner;
- are generous in their dealings with others, never trying to undercut or shortchange the other party;
- speak their opinions boldly and in a way that can be heard fully by those to whom they speak;
- choose their timing carefully.

Abigail used her power in a godly way to conduct transactions. Jezebel used this same power in an ungodly way.

....
The Unrighteous Use of Transaction Power

Jezebel was the daughter of Ethbaal, king of the Sidonians. The Sidonians lived in what is now Lebanon, south of Beirut. The Sidonians were rebuked repeatedly by the prophets for their idolatry and moral laxity. These people of Phoenician descent were ardent worshipers of Baal, the prevailing cult among Israel's enemies. Baal worship was always associated with a great deal of pomp and ceremony. Temples were erected to Baal, as well as thousands of altars. Ritualistic sacrifices were conducted by thousands of priests. These sacrifices sometimes included physical mutilation and even human sacrifice.

Jezebel brought her worship practices with her when she became the wife of Ahab, king of Samaria. (See 1 Kings 16:31.) Ahab built a temple to Baal in Samaria.

A man named Naboth owned a vineyard next to the king's palace, and Ahab wanted it so he could turn it into a vegetable garden. He said to Naboth, "Give me your vineyard . . . and for it I will give you a vineyard better than it. Or, if it seems good to you, I will give you its worth in money." Ahab declined the offer, stating, "The LORD forbid that I should give the inheritance of my fathers to you!" (See 1 Kings 21:2–3.)

His feelings hurt, Ahab went home to sulk. He lay down on his bed, turned his face to the wall, and refused to eat. Jezebel asked him why his spirit was so sullen and he told her what had happened.

Now from her perspective and experience as a Sidonian princess, Jezebel believed that whatever a king wanted, a king got. Kings ruled with absolute power in Sidon—certainly her father did—and her concept of a king was that of a man who had absolute control over all the people in his land. Indeed, the citizenry existed to serve the king and to do his will and pleasure.

Ahab, however, had a different concept of what it meant to

be a king. From the Hebrew standpoint, a king was to serve his people. Honest and equitable transactions needed to be forged. Ahab did not believe he had any right to Naboth's property, only the privilege to make a request and to exchange land for either money or better land. Jezebel's and Ahab's opinions about kingship couldn't have been more opposite.

Jezebel saw her husband's response as a sign of weakness. She said to him, "I will give you the vineyard of Naboth the Jezreelite." And so, she wrote letters in Ahab's name, sealed them with his seal, and sent the letters to the elders and nobles who lived in the city with Naboth. She advised in the letters that the leaders were to proclaim a holy fast and then seat Naboth with high honor among the people. They were to plant two scoundrels in the crowd to bear false witness against Naboth, claiming that he had blasphemed God and the king. On the basis of those two false witnesses, the elders and noblemen were to take Naboth out of the city and stone him to death.

Jezebel acted without consulting her husband, but she acted not to secure what was rightfully hers, both legally and morally, but to gain what was *not* rightfully hers. She did not make her own petition on his behalf, but rather, she wrote letters in Ahab's name.

Nevertheless, her plot worked. Naboth was stoned to death and Ahab, at Jezebel's instigation, took possession of Naboth's vineyard.

This was just the beginning. The Old Testament writers conclude that there was "no one like Ahab who sold himself to do wickedness in the sight of the LORD, because Jezebel his wife stirred him up" (1 Kings 21:25). In others words, Jezebel continually provoked Ahab to engage in illegal, unrighteous transactions. The Bible calls what she did sin, and states it as the reason for her violent and gruesome death.

The power to transact is not at issue here. The motive behind the use of that power, and the ends toward which it was directed are at issue. Jezebel had the same power as Abigail, but she was motivated *by* evil to use her transaction power *for* evil.

Abigail became the wife of a king for her righteous use of transaction power. Jezebel was the wife of a king and died for her unrighteous use of this power!

....

Bible Principles for Transactions

Apart from righteous motives and intent, the Bible has numerous other principles that govern righteous transactions.

One principle is that believers are not to be "unequally yoked" with others. Yoking is a term that most directly relates to business and work—specifically, the pulling of carts and plows by oxen. We are to pull together for common causes with fellow believers, those who are like-minded.

The Israelites were admonished to keep their weights and scales balanced honestly and not to charge interest from their fellow Israelites. A fellow Israelite was always to be given a way or means of honorably repaying an indebtedness. God's people are told repeatedly to stay out of debt, and should they accrue debt, to repay it as quickly as possible.

These and many other general principles regarding transactions are never gender limited. Women and men are to follow the same Bible commandments and principles.

Two of the main Bible admonitions regarding transactions are related to greed and to competition. Believers are to complement, support, and encourage one another. They are to be part of the same body. Competition is out. Cooperation is in.

As believers conduct transactions, they are to do so with a concern for meeting the needs of the body of Christ as a whole. In the Old Testament, the standard of giving is the tithe, one tenth. This giving is to come off the top, or be the "first fruits." No God-fearing person is to amass great wealth at the expense of the poor. Greed is out. Giving is in. Believers are admonished to be generous and cheerful givers.

As a whole, the power to transact must be taken as a derivative of the covenant-making power of God. Covenants seek to bind people together into mutually beneficial relationships. God's covenant with humankind is a binding, committed relationship. Men and women make treaties or sign contracts in an effort to make binding, lasting, permanent agreements.

The righteous use of transaction necessitates that these agreements and relationships be fully in keeping with God's laws and commandments. We, therefore, are not to enter into transactions of any kind that will harm a fellow human being, and particularly, a fellow believer.

We are to conduct all of our business transactions as if we are entering into a transaction with a representative of the Lord God Almighty. Would a person knowingly cheat God . . . steal from Him, rob Him, attempt to con Him, be dishonest with Him? It's not likely.

We sometimes attempt to bribe God, however. And often we attempt to barter with Him—"I'll do this for You, if You'll do this for me."

In conducting our transactions in a godly manner, we must recognize that we can never give our way, or buy our way, into God's mercy and grace. He has already extended to us the opportunity to enter into the fullness of His presence and power, according to rules and protocol that He has prescribed. That protocol is based upon humbly receiving by faith what God offers to give. God's gifts cannot be purchased, bartered, or negotiated. We have only one transaction option regarding His forgiveness and the gifts of His Spirit: to accept them or reject them.

Still, God has given us as part of our divine endowment of His image, the ability to enter into and to form binding, legal transactions with one another. We are to do so with a full awareness that our transactions are a manifestation of our Christianity.

We cannot be business people Monday through Friday, family members on Saturday, and church people on Sunday. All of our transactions are to reflect the transforming power of Christ's Holy Spirit at work in us.

....

Transaction Power on an International Scale

Another Bible woman noted for her power of transaction is the Queen of Sheba. This woman was faced with a problem of international proportions. King Solomon had built a number of fortresses across the desert sands of Arabia that effectively controlled the travel of caravans, and thus, the trade of spices, fabrics, and precious gems from nation to nation. Solomon's "gate-keepers" in the desert exacted high taxes, what we would call tariffs today, for the privilege of safe passage. And nobody could do much about it except pay up and proceed with caution.

The Queen of Sheba decided to address this matter head-on and went to meet with Solomon personally. The Bible tells us that she had heard of Solomon's fame "concerning the name of the Lord." In other words, she had heard not only of what he was doing with his fortresses in the desert, but also that God was on his side. She went to Solomon to "test him with hard questions."

The impression we may have drawn of the Queen of Sheba from childhood storybooks is that of a pretty young veiled maiden on something of a sight-seeing tour to the big city.

How false that image is! The Queen of Sheba had to have been a tough monarch. Out of concern for her own nation and its financial welfare, she set out on a journey to face the man whom she may very well have perceived as an enemy. She was obviously a woman who had great authority in her homeland. No queen would dare leave her nation for several months without strongly believing that she was impervious to an attempted over-throw in her absence. She was a woman who had things solidly under control on the homefront.

The journey she undertook was overland, which was no easy journey in ancient times. She traveled as part of a great caravan, over the hot desert sands, day after day and week after week. There was no hot shower or light left burning for her at a motel each night. There were no truck stops where she could grab a quick bite to eat in an air-conditioned café. Women rarely traveled by caravan. The experience was too hard physically, and too dangerous.

The Queen of Sheba, however, was willing to face this challenge, and she obviously commanded the respect of her own security forces and entourage. No mention is made of *maidservants* being with her, only servants.

Once in Jerusalem, the queen spoke openly to Solomon "all that was in her heart." She held nothing back. Part of what she said no doubt included her concerns, her frustrations, her perceptions, her doubts, and her opinions regarding his control of the desert route. She asked him every question she wanted to ask.

Now a king such as Solomon would have had absolute control over a conversation of this type. With a mere flick of his wrist or nod of his head, the audience with this queen would have been over. He need not have greeted her or spent time with her. He owed her nothing. Furthermore, kings rarely take kindly to questions. Questions are almost always regarded by people in high political authority as threatening in some way, or as a sign of disrespect. It's easy to imagine a king raging at a foreign visitor, "How dare you question what I do or why I do what I do!" We shouldn't forget that this *woman* was asking hard questions of a *man* . . . something that has never been easy for a man to take in any culture at any time in history.

The Queen of Sheba obviously had a presence and a bearing that commanded Solomon's respect. He answered all of her questions with detailed explanations. He invited her to see his entire palace and to have dinner with him. His answers and his tour left her in a state that the Bible describes this way: "There was no more spirit in her." The implication is that there was no more fight left in her. This feisty monarch was satisfied that Solomon had not only the power to construct his fortresses, but also the wisdom and material wealth to manage them and keep them in place, and that his reasoning and spiritual resolve couldn't be bested.

She concluded, "Because the LORD has loved Israel forever, therefore He made you king, to do justice and righteousness" (1 Kings 10:9). She was saying to him, "I trust you also to do the right thing and to play fair."

The queen gave generous and precious gifts to Solomon—gold, spices, precious stones, and great quantities of valuable almug wood. The servants of Solomon had never seen such an abundance of spices or such wonderful wood.

In return, Solomon gave to the queen "all she desired, whatever she asked," in addition to royal gifts that matched in value what the queen had given to him (1 Kings 10:13). In other words, the queen got the international deal she had been seeking. We don't know the details of that treaty, but we do know that the Queen of Sheba went to Jerusalem with an agenda, and she went home with her agenda accomplished.

Do women have the power to conduct transactions? The Queen of Sheba certainly did. She knew what she wanted. She knew where to go to get what she wanted. She wasn't afraid to make the trek to get there. She boldly made her requests known. Each of these is a vitally important point to consider as we think about the transactions we desire to make in our lives personally, professionally, and on behalf of God's kingdom.

Do we really know what we want? Until we know, we shouldn't go. Once we know what we want, we need to know where to go to get it. That may be to a place. It may be to a person.

Then, we need to make certain we aren't intimidated by

either the place or the person, or the trip to get there. Sometimes that trip is as simple as an elevator ride to the top floor. Sometimes it's a trip to the downtown courthouse. Sometimes it's a trip to the altar rail.

When the time comes for us to present our case, we need to be prepared—our questions in line, our points and requests succinctly and clearly stated, and our research verified.

We need to ask boldly for what we want. To ask boldly does not mean to ask belligerently, angrily, or emotionally. Bold requests can be made graciously, politely, and in a well-modulated voice.

We have no indication that the Queen of Sheba behaved in anything but a gracious and appealing manner. Solomon, a connoisseur of women, probably wouldn't have given the Queen of Sheba the time of day if she hadn't been a master of gracious seduction as well as a master of gracious transaction.

Be Prepared When Opportunities Arise

Both Esther and the Queen of Sheba went to key decision makers to conduct transactions. Wise women are prepared should a top decision maker come their way!

For a number of years, I reported directly to the chief executive officer of a fairly large organization. My vice-president's office was next door to his for three years, a matter of much concern to a number of people in the organization who perceived that I had many more encounters with the boss than I actually had. This particular man did not have an open-door policy, and I rarely initiated a meeting with him unless a matter was urgent. What happened with far greater frequency was that my boss made unannounced and unexpected end-of-the-day visits to my office.

His custom was to walk in, sit down on a chair next to my desk, prop his feet up on my desk, and then say, "Tell me everything you know." Implied was the added phrase, "in twenty-five words or less before I leave today."

The first time, he caught me by surprise and I didn't have much to say. Every other time, however, I was prepared.

"I know that, with your permission, I need to . . ."

"I know that some good things are happening in Department X . . ."

"I know that you need to commend Person Y for his accomplishment . . ."

"I know that we need to do something about Situation Z. I have three ideas for your consideration . . ."

And sometimes I said, "I know a new joke . . ." or "I know something nice that was said about you in secret."

It was from this man that I learned several key things about conducting transactions:

- Don't bring up a matter unless you are sure the key decision maker is ready to hear about it. But, always be prepared should the decision maker bring up a matter.

- Don't go to any meeting unprepared. Insist on having a copy of an agenda in advance of a meeting whenever possible. Anticipate as much as you can about the issues that are going to be discussed. Prepare yourself as thoroughly as possible for possible decisions. Have your statistics and facts in good order.

- Have an opinion. When asked what you think about something or what you know, have something to say that is constructive, positive, and problem-solving.

- Have your facts straight and well-substantiated. Don't deal in rumor. Relay only information you can support.

- If you don't have anything to say that is helpful, keep quiet. The bearer of negative tidings is usually considered to be "bad news" herself.

- As much as you are selling ideas and opinions, you are selling yourself. In many cases, a decision maker will trust you, believe in you, or make a decision because of who you are as a person, even if he knows very little about what it is that you are requesting or suggesting. Earn a decision maker's trust, don't betray it, and make sure you ask or suggest only those things that are truly important to you. Don't waste your precious reputation on trivia.

....

Businesswomen in the New Testament

Do we find examples of women conducting transactions in the New Testament? Several come to my mind readily.

Lydia is called a "seller of purple from the city of Thyatira" (Acts 16:14). To be a seller of purple was to be involved in the manufacturing of textiles and to be engaged in the trade of purple dye and purple fabrics. Lydia was prosperous to the point where she had a house in Philippi, which apparently was large enough so that she could conveniently host Paul and his brethren. We have no mention of a husband for Lydia, so we can assume that she was a wealthy woman as the result of her own talent and work. Her home was the likely meeting place of the church in Philippi, which is one of the most faithful and generous churches noted in the New Testament.

Mary Magdalene, Joanna the wife of Chuza (Herod's steward), and Susanna are named among a group of women who "provided for [Jesus] with their substance." These followers of Jesus apparently had control over certain monies, sums that they gave to Jesus to meet His earthly needs as He ministered. They apparently worked as a team of women who knew each other and coordinated their efforts and gifts.

Priscilla worked with her husband Aquila in the tent making industry. Their names are nearly always linked in scriptural references, and the implication is that Paul worked alongside the two of them.

Martha, sister of Lazarus and Mary, appears to have been the homeowner of the place in Bethany where Jesus frequently stayed. Luke 10:38 tells us, "Martha welcomed Him into her house." Every example we have of Martha depicts her as practical and very much concerned with getting the job done.

Each of these women had power that she used for the benefit of God's kingdom. Lydia was an integral part of the early church, using her home and her resources to further God's work in Philippi. Mary Magdalene, Joanna, and Susanna gave of their money to fund Jesus' ministry. Priscilla used her position as a platform for teaching and sharing the gospel. Martha used her resources to be a superlative hostess to Jesus and His disciples.

Each of these women had the power to make her giving count. So did the widow who gave two mites. So did the woman who anointed Jesus' feet with oil and tears and dried His feet with her hair. So did Mary, who anointed Jesus' head and feet with her costly perfume, an action Jesus regarded as symbolic of His anointing for burial.

As a Christian woman, you have the power to make your giving count. You have something to give. Lay claim to your fair share of your family's resources. Achsah, Caleb's daughter, boldly asked her father for a greater inheritance than traditionally would have been given to her. She requested a blessing and springs of water to make fertile the land her father had already given her. Caleb responded by giving her both the upper and lower springs! (See Josh. 15:16–19.) I know of no example in the Scriptures where a woman is completely and *righteously* stripped of all ability to give.

You should be able to give to your church and to godly causes according to your own volition and conviction. Your ability to give is linked to your ability to receive. You need to give personally so you can receive personally.

Phoebe delivered Paul's letter to Rome. Tabitha made garments that were distributed to needy saints. John Mark's mother hosted the early church at her home in Jerusalem. Women in the first century were an integral part of all aspects of the life of the church—giving and receiving, buying and selling, going and doing, teaching and prophesying, and winning converts through their lives and witness.

The Power to Transact Business in the Kingdom

Consider again the points made throughout this chapter about the nature of righteous transactions:

- Have a willingness to make transactions. This willingness includes some risk, perhaps of resources and nearly always of reputation.
- Have a clear goal in mind, and conduct any necessary research related to it.
- Get the best possible advice.
- Deal only with the final decision maker.
- Know how to value things properly so that you can be fair and even-handed in your transactions.
- Be generous wherever possible.
- Engage in whatever aspects of business are necessary in order to complete a transaction satisfactorily.
- Work with others to reach mutually acceptable goals.
- Work for ends that benefit the whole, not just one individual.
- Be willing to speak and make requests boldly in ways that the requests can be heard and acted upon.

With these principles in mind, let's consider two key transaction questions about the role of women in God's kingdom. Think like a person capable of engaging in high-powered, high-level transactions as you frame your own responses!

Question #1:
What territory in the world does evil control?

Rather than think in terms of conquering evil by means of overt warfare (something we'll address in a discussion about spiritual warfare later in this book), think in terms of a leveraged buyout of the territory that the evil one currently holds!

Don't destroy. Purchase!

Don't alienate and confront. Instead, take over control!

Don't do battle. Do business!

For example, is there an area in your city where evil reigns? It may be a strip of buildings or a particular street. It might be a certain club or place of business. What can you do to redeem that territory for Christ?

You might buy it out.

You might surround it with good and build a buffer zone around it so that those with evil desires no longer feel comfortable traveling to and from this place.

You might work to build good relationships with the owners of the property.

You might seek to gain controlling interest in the enterprise so that you can vote for changes.

You might create a wonderful master plan with others that turns the disaster zone into a place of beauty, purpose, and productivity.

There are hundreds of possible ways that you can engage in a transaction that will remove the enemy. This isn't doing business *with* the enemy. It's buying out the enemy's controlling interest!

Is there a part of your child's school that you'd like to see redeemed and made accessible or comfortable for your child? If so, what do you want to see happen?

Who is the top decision maker?

Have others been through this? Whom can you consult?

Whom can you ask to join you, or to contribute to your cause? What mutual plan can you lay?

Where do you need to go to make your requests known boldly? How much effort will be required, and are you willing to make it?

Evil exists to a great extent because believers are unwilling to confront it or resist it.

Question #2:
What can I do to make the territory held
by God's people safer or more secure?

We are told repeatedly in the Scriptures to guard ourselves and to keep ourselves from evil. The Psalms frequently refer to God as a fortress, a rock of refuge, a safe place.

Even as we seek to gain control of enemy territory, we need to make certain that our own territory is made secure.

The Church is not intended to be a barricaded shelter or a self-imposed prison. It is, however, intended to be a place of refuge for people who need a safe place. It is a place for those who are suffering to recover, regroup, or heal.

What more might you and other godly women you know do to create a more comforting, welcoming, and nurturing environment for those who are hurting in your community, or even in your church? Do you have a place, a program, friends, or assistance to offer to those who are battered, abused, going through a divorce, grieving, feeling the impact of a loss, unemployed, in need of shelter or food? You may not be able to tackle all the needs at once, but you can tackle one need at a time until all needs are met!

Think in terms of transactions. What transactions can you undertake to create a place of refuge, comfort, wise counsel, and love for those who are hurting?

Take it on as a "business" challenge. How do you sell the

idea to others? What's your niche in the "marketplace of need"? Whom can you call? What goals can you set? How can you become organized to meet this need? What obstacles stand in your way? How can you address them?

Christians are called to manifest faith through good works, and especially through good works that benefit fellow believers.

....

Women Have What It Takes to Conduct Effective Transactions

Part of an effective transaction is the ability to focus your efforts. You may think you can't fight evil and create refuge simultaneously. But look at it this way: when you're creating refuge, when you're doing something good for people, aren't you fighting evil? Certainly the ideal takeover of enemy territory is to turn something evil into something that benefits and blesses others.

You may not be able to undertake such a goal alone. But you probably know others you can call to help you.

You have the authority and the ability to conduct righteous transactions. The real question is, will you use that power for good and against evil?

6

....

The
Power to
Train

For millennia, women have exercised their power to teach and to train. Mothers do so every day. Countless women are also teachers of some type, either in their professions or on a voluntary basis.

More than 90 percent of the elementary school teachers in the United States are women. An even higher percentage of elementary Sunday school teachers are female. The majority of secondary school teachers are women. And the number of women teaching in colleges is growing in direct proportion to the number of women who are earning master's and doctoral degrees.

Even in nations where women are culturally limited from holding key leadership positions, both in the secular society and in the church, women are nearly always allowed to teach children and other women. In other words, women may not be allowed to teach "men," but they are allowed to teach boys, as well as the girls who will become the wives, mothers, sisters, aunts, and grandmothers of both present and future husbands, fathers, brothers, uncles, and grandfathers!

The Scriptures say that Priscilla joined her husband Aquila in explaining the fullness of the gospel of Jesus Christ to Apollos, who had a great evangelistic preaching ministry in the first century. (See Acts 18:26.)

The Bible says women have the ability and the authority to teach. Perhaps more than at any time in history women today have the privilege of exercising the spiritual gift of teaching.

Training Involves More Than Teaching

Teaching is only one aspect of training. Teaching specifically involves the mental components of training, including such things as perception enhancement, conceptualization, vocabulary building, memorization, problem solving, decision making, rule learning, principle application, and logical reasoning.

Training also has a behavioral component—the "doing" aspect. Training includes not only learning information, but also applying information to life.

When a person trains another person, she requires that person to engage in certain behaviors repeatedly, from setting the family dining table to reciting multiplication tables. Training involves repetition until the behavior becomes internalized as a habit.

The Scripture also authorizes women to train. Parents, both mothers and fathers, are admonished in Proverbs 22:6 to "Train up a child in the way he should go, and when he is old he will not depart from it."

Deuteronomy 6:6–9, the classic passage in the Scriptures about parental teaching, says:

> "And these words which I command you today shall be in your heart. You shall teach them diligently to your children, and shall talk of them when you sit in your house, when you walk by the way, when you lie down, and when you rise up. You shall bind them as a sign on your hand, and they shall be as frontlets between your eyes. You shall write them on the doorposts of your house and on your gates."

This word is given to mothers as well as fathers. The first half of this command from God relates to teaching—around-the-clock explaining, exhibiting, and rehearsing mentally and verbally the things of God. The second half of the command relates to the behavioral aspects of training: bind and write. The binding refers to what the parents do with the law in their own lives. This binding doesn't relate to the children, as some parents seem to think. Some parents insist that their children *always* remember and *always* behave. That isn't what this passage implies, however. The writing refers to how the flow of teaching is controlled within the family. Both binding and writing will be covered more fully later.

Deuteronomy 11:18–21 repeats this command about training, and it provides a little more information about the prescribed teaching method. This passage also links the commands about training to a great reward:

> "Therefore you shall lay up these words of mine in your heart and in your soul, and bind them as a sign on your hand, and they shall be as frontlets between your eyes. You shall teach them to your children, speaking of them when you sit in your house, when you walk by the way, when you lie down, and when you rise up. And you shall write them on the doorposts of your house and on your gates, that your days and the days of your children may be multiplied in the land of which the LORD swore to your fathers to give them, like the days of the heavens above the earth."

What Is the Teaching Philosophy?

Essentially, the teacher must believe and do what she teaches. There is to be no inconsistency between what a woman tells others to do and what she does in her own life. She cannot ask others to believe what she doesn't believe.

We've all heard the phrase, "Do as I say, not as I do." It's not scriptural! We've also heard, "Those who do, do, and those who can't, teach." Also not scriptural.

The Lord requires that we teach others only what we believe and do in our own lives. This does not mean, of course, that we will not fail sometimes. The fact is, we will fail. No one is perfect in obedience to Christ. Yet, even in our failure, we are to repent, to seek God's forgiveness and help in changing our ways, and then to will to do a better job of obeying in the future.

What Is the Teaching Methodology?

The teaching methodology has three parts. The first is near nonstop talking, listening, and conversing, from sunup to sundown.

Communication Parents are to give their children something of a running commentary on life, pointing out how each aspect of life relates to God's commandments. We explain to our children why we do certain things. We answer their questions as fully as we can. We make ourselves available to our children to explore life *with them*. We are curious and awed by the natural world that God has created. We ask questions of ourselves, of our children, and of God. We talk to God about our feelings and ideas, and we ask God to reveal to us what it is that He would have us do and say prior to making decisions. And we encourage our children to join in, each step of the way. Thus, we build into our children a continual reason for behaving in certain ways.

As a teenager once said to me, "There must have been a *whole* lot of communicatin' going on."

I suspect there was. And isn't that what we advise ourselves today when it comes to developing a solid relationship with our children and teens? Talk to them. Listen to them. Be available to them.

Activity and Application The second part of the methodology is the doing. We don't tell our children *about* certain behaviors. We engage in those behaviors with our children. We take them along. We explore with them. We play with them. We let them work with us, letting them try their hands at various skills, accommodating their mistakes and crude efforts just as our loving heavenly Father allows us to blunder along in helping Him build His kingdom.

The older a child grows, the more we allow him or her to participate fully in the doing of our lives—the chores, the decisions, the problem solving, the leadership.

Now for some parents this is going to sound very limiting. "Be with my children all the time? That's not possible." Well, the Scriptures say from getting-up time to going-to-bed time!

Some parents may feel limited because certain adult privileges seem to be precluded in this commandment. I suspect they are. Adults have come to assume that they have a privilege and right *not* to be innocent in certain areas. The Scriptures never give us the privilege to dabble in sin. In other words, what is right for you to see, hear, consume, and do should be right for your children to see, hear, consume, and do.

I recently read a nutrition book in which the author advised expectant mothers, "Don't take anything into your body that you wouldn't want to bottle feed or inject into your infant should you be holding your baby in your arms right now." I find that to be good advice for a parent at any age. The same applies to spiritual, mental, and emotional "food" as well as physical food.

That's what it means, in part, for the parent to bind God's commandments to her hands and to have them as "frontlets" between her eyes. We don't allow ourselves to see or touch anything that is forbidden by God. We stay pure. We think pure thoughts. We engage in righteous activities. We keep God and His laws continually in mind as we live our lives and make our choices.

Gatekeeping As much as parents teach and do with their children, they also are responsible for prohibiting their children from experiencing certain things.

The writer of Deuteronomy proclaims that the commands of God are to be "written" on the doors and gates of our homes. The

Jewish people adopted this practice literally, affixing statements of the law to the sides of their entrances in little containers called *mezuzah.*

While Christians don't have a custom like that, we still have the moral and spiritual responsibility of making certain that no evil crosses our threshold in either direction. That's an awesome responsibility, and one that many parents are going to find requires toughness.

Imagine that the laws of God surround our homes. Nothing goes in or out of our homes that isn't filtered through God's will and commandments. That's what this passage means! In a practical way, it means that

- nothing comes into our homes, in the way of literature, music, or people, that doesn't line up with God's Word; and
- nothing goes out of our homes, in the form of creative expression or work, that doesn't bring glory to God.

What an awesome task this is!

It means saying no when our children want to bring home a toy or a video or a CD that has a message that is contrary to God's Word. It means saying no to a child when she wants to bring home a friend who is an influence for evil. It means saying no to baby-sitters and guests who don't keep God's commandments. It means saying no to the entrance of an adult child should he or she rebel against the godly rules of the home. It also means that certain language and behaviors are not allowed within the home.

The specifics are going to be up to the individual's interpretation of various passages of the Scriptures, but if we do only that which we know with certainty to do, we'll still have plenty of commandments to follow!

Gulp. This takes fortitude. And as women, our hearts will often melt out of self-proclaimed love for our children. True love, however, demands that we train our children from early ages that certain things, behaviors, and influences are not allowed in our homes. We do this by example and by explaining. And we also do it by gatekeeping.

The child at sixteen is not going to understand a change in rules without a great deal of explanation and time spent with the parent. The child is certainly not going to understand gatekeeping that doesn't line up with a parent's expressed beliefs and behaviors.

Modeling The teaching methodology described in the Bible is that which educators today term *modeling*. The teacher models beliefs and behavior that a child copies. From the other side of the coin, a child copies only behavior and ideas he has seen and heard from a reliable source.

This method for teaching requires a great deal of personal involvement, which always entails some degree of vulnerability and risk. As believers, we must be willing to expose our faith to others.

It requires patience. Modeling is not hit-and-run teaching. It is a method of training that requires a great deal of time and frequent encounters. The lessons take place day in and day out. Patience, of course, requires a willingness to nurture even when a person would rather be doing something else. Patience requires sacrifice of self. As believers, we are called to sacrifice our own desires if it means benefit to others.

This model for teaching also requires a great deal of consistency. Beliefs must line up with actions. Words and deeds must be seamless. When that happens, the gatekeeping aspects of the teaching become automatic. Decisions related to keeping evil out of the home are seen in a context of beliefs and habits that are deeply ingrained. As such, they are not only tolerated, but also embraced.

The consistency must include both parents, of course. That's the Bible ideal. Two parents. Two "words of witness" to children in the establishment of truth in their lives. Two examples to follow. But . . . one set of rules, and only one God to love and serve.

When the biblical ideal isn't in place, a parent faces an extra challenge. And it's often with her own husband and regarding her own children that a woman must take a firm stance.

As long as a parent has responsibility for a child, a parent needs to have authority over that child. Mothers have a right to insist that their children obey them for as long as the children are supported by the parents.

The Scriptures give mothers authority to require obedience from their children. Ephesians 6:1–3 states, "Children, obey your parents in the Lord, for this is right. 'Honor your father and mother,' which is the first commandment with promise: 'that it may be well with you and you may live long on the earth.'"

If a husband insists that his wife not do certain things with the child, or insists that the wife not limit the child in certain ways that the wife believes are in keeping with God's commandments, then the husband must be willing to take full responsibility for the fate of the child. A wife should explain this to her husband in clear terms. If he will not allow his wife to have authority over the child in ways that are in keeping with God's Word, then he must not hold his wife responsible in the least for the future of the child. That's a tough line to hold. But it's essential.

Making this stand does two things. It lets a husband know that his wife is serious and committed to following God's rules in the home. It also lets the husband know that his wife believes a failure to follow God's commandments has serious consequences, which he must be willing to accept. If a wife issues an ultimatum, she must be prepared to stick by it, and be sure to present her husband with the full downside of consequences for which she will *not* be held responsible.

I know of one woman who put this statement into writing, and it was only when her husband saw it in black and white, had time to ponder her words, and was faced with the request to sign the document for placement in a safe-deposit box, that he agreed to allow her to establish godly principles as the hallmark of their home. He since has come into a wonderful relationship with Christ and is actually the more strict of the two parents.

In taking such a gatekeeping stance, a wife needs to be very certain that the rules and principles she wishes to exact in the home are in keeping with God's commandments. She can underline the passages where certain commandments appear in God's Word, and make certain that she has the commandments in context. These underlined passages can serve as a quick reference should disputes arise about God's commandments.

If a husband remains unconvinced of his wife's interpretation of certain commandments, she should consult commentaries or other reliable sources of information, and present those arguments to her husband, letting him read various interpretations or statements for himself from original sources. This practice should not be done in the presence of the children. This is an issue best kept private between husband and wife.

A wife can and should, however, openly discuss certain commandments with her older children and teenagers, letting them read God's Word for themselves.

As I have watched a number of women take this stand through the years, I have met only one man who was willing to take on the sole responsibility of his children's fate. This particular man refused to allow his wife to discipline their children, to talk to them about God's commandments, to prohibit the entrance of certain posters, music, and alcohol into their home, or to use the word *sin* in their home. He declared himself willing to take on the full responsibility for his children. Today, however, he desires to give part of that responsibility back and to make his wife co-responsible for the fact that their son is using cocaine and their daughter is promiscuous.

Some men may question their wife's resolve, but most men

not only value such resolve but are also willing to openly stand by their wives as they exact certain behavior from their children—even men who don't proclaim to know Christ.

In all, mothers train their children through a thorough expression of their own faith in both word and deed. Mothers give examples to their children that much of life is related to *not* doing certain things. Choices in life cover acts of commission—choosing what to do—and of omission, choosing what not to do.

What Are the Rewards of This Teaching?

Great, awesome, and eternal rewards are promised to those who teach and learn in this manner. We are told that both our children and we ourselves will live longer—yes, even eternally. In other words, our children will make the right decisions that lead to long and satisfying lives on this earth. They will also make the right choices and decisions that will secure eternal life for them.

Grading and Evaluating Many types of teaching involve grades and evaluations. Modeling does not. Modeling involves judging behaviors in advance of their adoption and performance, choosing those behaviors that are righteous, and performing them. The person learning behaviors acquires them as habit. If good behaviors and right decision making become habits, the teacher has succeeded. If they don't, the teacher has failed. If there's any evaluating and grading involved in modeling, it's evaluating and grading of the teacher, not the student.

In many ways this is the exact opposite of the way the school systems operate. Students are graded, not teachers. The Scriptures call for the reverse. Those who teach others are held to a higher standard.

From a biblical standpoint, we fail as teachers if our students do not emulate our example. What a sobering thought. On the other hand, when our students succeed, our lives are enriched and extended. What a glorious possibility!

........,..................

Training Adults and Other People's Children

What about training adults or other people's children? The same principles apply.

A woman should teach only what she believes to be true. If she teaches what she doesn't believe to be true, she is a hypocrite, and others will surely recognize her as one sooner or later.

She should do and live by what she teaches. If she can't live out a certain principle, she shouldn't punish others for failing to live it out in their lives. This should not be taken as a license to sin. I'm not saying, "If you can't keep a commandment, don't proclaim it as a commandment." A commandment of God is a commandment of God. It stands whether we obey it or not. We should proclaim God's commandments and teach and explain them to others. To admit our personal failure is not, however, giving license to others to fail.

When the scribes and Phariseees brought a woman caught in adultery to Jesus, they argued that the woman should be stoned in accordance with God's law. Jesus replied, "He who is without sin among you, let him throw a stone at her first" (John 8:7). Nobody did. One by one, the accusers walked away, interestingly, from the oldest to the youngest. In the end, all realized they had sinned and were in no position to punish.

Jesus asked the woman, "Has no one condemned you?" She said, "No one, Lord." And Jesus said to her, "Neither do I condemn you; go and sin no more." (See John 8:3–11.) Had her accusers stayed around to hear this exchange, in all likelihood, Jesus would have turned to them and said to them also, "Go and sin no more."

If we must be perfect in our beliefs or behavior before we teach, none of us would qualify. Still, we can and must strive for this consistency.

Finally, we must shut the doors of our classrooms to evil.

We must name evil for what it is, deny its presence in our midst, and refuse to teach where evil is made welcome.

As in parenthood, a teacher has authority for her students as long as she has responsibility for them. In the case of parents leaving their children in your care at school, Sunday school, Scout or club meetings, athletic practices, or for fine art and other private lessons, a teacher can assume that parents are giving her authority over their children because they are holding her responsible for teaching them certain information or skills. If she has any doubts about this, she should talk to the parents and if need be, have a written agreement with them. A teacher should discuss the limits of her authority and responsibility. This is critically important if she is asked to assume the position of a caregiver for young children, perhaps in a day care or after-school care situation. She should know what the parents want and don't want her to do. If she can't conscientiously abide by their wishes, she shouldn't take the job.

When teaching adults, a teacher should let them know that she has no direct responsibility for them. Her responsibility is to the Lord—to be faithful in what she teaches about Him and to respond to the class as He may ask her to respond. At the same time, she should assume that she has no authority over her adult students. Major problems occur when an adult teacher takes on responsibility for and assumes authority over other adults. Cults often use this model. A teacher shouldn't fall into this trap.

A teacher should openly admit to her adult students that they are responsible for checking out everything she teaches against the principles of God's Word. They should be reading and studying God's Word for themselves. Students should know that they are responsible for developing their own relationship with the Lord Jesus Christ and for learning how to listen to the wise counsel of the Holy Spirit as He speaks to them.

What about other adults who come to stay or live in a woman's home? If it's the woman's home, and she has the legal and financial responsibility for the home, she has the privilege of making up the rules. This is true even if she charges rent to another person. The home is intended to be an outpost of heaven, operating according to heaven's rules and regulations just as an embassy in a foreign land operates according to the rules and regulations of its homeland. A woman responsible for the home is Christ's ambassador-in-residence. She has the authority to exact and enact the presiding rules.

....

Impacting the Next Generation

For a number of years in our nation, the jobs of teacher, nurse, and secretary were labeled women's jobs. For that reason, some women today disdain the job of teacher. They don't want to be limited to being a teacher.

As a teacher by training, profession, and vocation, I strongly believe in the nobility and the importance of teaching as a profession. Teaching allows a person to impact the next generation in a profound way. In many ways, it is our teachers who "create" the next generation. They may not procreate the bodies, minds, and souls of their students, but they greatly impact the level of health, the depth of ideas, the breadth of behavior, and the height of aspirations in those they teach.

Perhaps the greatest impact a woman can have toward the betterment of the world, the growth of the kingdom of God, and the enhancement of her own privileges as a woman, is to teach others, and especially boys and girls, what it means to be a genuine Christian—one who embodies the life of Christ in thought, word, and deed.

Consider some of the great women teachers in the Bible. Mrs. Noah certainly taught her three sons the right way to live. They didn't rebel against their father, Noah, and against what he believed and did. They didn't pursue evil, as everyone else in their generation was doing. As a result, their lives were spared, and they were given the awesome task of reviving a flood-ravaged world.

Jochebed must have been a wonderful teacher. Her son Moses became the lawgiver and leader of his people. Her son Aaron became the priest of his people. And her daughter Miriam was a prophetess to her people. Where did these children learn what to say and how to live? From Jochebed and her husband. Even after Moses was taken into the Egyptian court, Jochebed was allowed entrance to be the nursemaid to her son. In that role, she taught him so well that he never departed from an affection and affinity for the Hebrew people.

Jedidah influenced her son Josiah for good. Josiah was only eight years old when he became king. Amon, his father, was murdered by conspirators and it was up to Jedidah, the daughter of Adaiah of Bozkath, to train her son. The Scriptures tell us that Josiah "did what was right in the sight of the Lord . . . ; he did not turn aside to the right hand or to the left" (2 Kings 22:2). Josiah repaired the Temple and when the scrolls of the law were found among the ruins, Josiah ordered that they be read aloud to the people. He led the nation in repentance, and on his people's behalf, he renewed the covenant with the Lord.

Hannah dedicated her son Samuel to the Lord and gave him to the high priest for service when Samuel was a very young child. Samuel was the priest of the Hebrew people for many years and anointed both King Saul and King David.

The greatest influence these women had was not on their adult peers, but on the future. They had a great impact for good through the lives of those they taught and trained.

The same holds for women today. As teachers of God's principles, they may not know great fame or fortune. They may not be recognized fully or rewarded even adequately for the work they do. But they have great influence and a great opportunity to impact this world for good.

Who knows what young boy or girl in the class, or what

adult who sits under the teacher, will become a missionary, a pastor, an evangelist, an apostle, a prophet . . . or a teacher! Who knows what idea will spark a student toward acceptance of Jesus Christ as Savior and Lord? Who knows what word a teacher speaks or what example she gives by her very life, will inspire a young person or a young believer to grow to full maturity in Christ and to make contributions for good and not evil in our world?

....

The Many Avenues of Teaching

Countless avenues for teaching are available to women today. School teaching and Sunday school teaching are only two avenues. Teachers also are employed in industry. Many companies have training programs or continuing education divisions. Teachers are sent abroad to teach English and other skills in humanitarian efforts and as part of business enterprises. Some teachers write manuals or instructional materials, and private tutors are employed for specialized purposes in virtually every walk of life. Any of these avenues can include an opportunity for sharing Christ.

Are you a tutor to someone? Then you no doubt will have a wonderful opportunity at some point to share your faith with this person. Be open to that possibility. Seize the moment when it comes.

Are you being sent overseas to work with foreign students? They'll be interested in knowing what you believe. Even in highly restrictive environments, foreign teachers are often asked to explain the religious aspects of American culture, or to interpret the behavior of certain believers.

Have you been asked to write text materials? What contributions from Christians, or which Christian principles and teachings, might you include in your presentation? You can remain objective as you do this. Facts can be just as potent as opinions when the name of Christ is introduced into areas where it isn't necessarily expected. Even if your statement is edited out, you will at least have conveyed something to your editor!

The point is this: Be bold in your witness for Christ as a teacher, regardless of what you are teaching or who your students are. Let your words about Christ flow naturally from your beliefs and your behavior. Be true to yourself and true to Christ. Few can argue with facts and opinions that are presented in that context, in the love of Christ, and with an intent to inform and present rather than to coerce. The Holy Spirit can do the persuading, if you will do the presenting.

Are women authorized to train? Yes.

Do they have ability to train? Yes.

Do you as a woman have the power to train? *Yes, you do!* Train in a way that honors your Lord and Savior. And be willing to train others whenever the opportunity presents itself.

7

....

The
Power to
Witness

Women have the power to be Christ's witnesses on the earth. Although there has been much discussion regarding the right of women to preach, teach, or fill leadership roles in the Church, nothing in the Scriptures precludes women from living out the gospel. The Scriptures proclaim that *all* believers, male and female, have great responsibility and privilege as God's children on earth.

Nowhere in Scripture are women precluded from the redemptive work of Christ Jesus. Women are to be forgiven, redeemed, renewed, baptized, confirmed in the faith, sanctified, justified, and filled with the Holy Spirit, according to broad definitions for virtually all of these concepts. Women are recipients of all of the gifts of the Holy Spirit and are vessels through whom these gifts might be poured. They are called to bear fully the fruit of the Holy Spirit. (See Gal. 5:22–23.) They are to become Christlike and be full members of the universal Church, the body of Christ. They are challenged to keep the commandments of God, to show love to one another, and to honor Christ in all things. Women have the full privilege of becoming Christians, and thus, of bearing Christ's presence and power into the world as His witnesses.

Women have two types of power when it comes to witnessing. They have the power to *be* a witness through the development and manifestation of godly character to all who know them. And, they have the power to *give* a witness, to verbally proclaim what Christ Jesus has done in their lives.

. . . .

Women Are Called to Be Ambassadors

The Scriptures liken the godly person's role on earth to that of an ambassador. First and foremost, ambassadors are members of their own nations, not of the nations to which they have been sent.

The Scriptures tell us that as believers we are full residents of heaven. Our home there is our eternal home. It is securely and eternally ours. We are residents of heaven even though we do not live there bodily and have not yet visited our true home. As residents, we are subject to the laws and protocol of heaven. Our residency on earth is likened to that of sojourners and wanderers, of aliens in a strange place.

All ambassadors must keep the laws of their own nation first and foremost, and then also keep the laws of their host nation. We, too, are to follow this pattern. Our primary allegiance is to the commandments of God. Secondarily, we obey the laws of our earthly nation and follow the rules and dictates of those whom the Lord has placed in authority over us.

Ambassadors, however, virtually always keep the cultural practices of their homeland within the walls of the embassy. They do not adopt the cultural practices and norms of their host land; rather, they attempt to teach and to share their cultural practices with those in the land to which they have been assigned. Within the embassy, the protocol, customs, and traditions are those of the ambassador's homeland. As believers, regardless of the culture outside the walls of our embassies—our homes and home churches—we keep the customs and traditions of heaven as the norm within our embassies.

Second, an ambassador does not negotiate or enter into contractual agreements with those in the host nation according to his or her own desires or on the basis of his or her own position. An ambassador is subject to the leadership of the homeland. We, too, are always subject to the leadership of heaven. We are subject to the will of God the Father.

Third, an ambassador's residence is fully protected by the ambassador's homeland. An ambassador has the right and privilege under international law to call for military assistance from the homeland to ensure his or her safety and the well-being of both embassy residents and property. We as ambassadors for Christ, who lives and reigns supreme in heaven, have the privilege and right to call our Leader and request assistance from heavenly troops. We do this through prayer.

Fourth, ambassadors enjoy certain immunity and receive certain privileges, such as special secure mail delivery and secrecy for monetary transactions. As Christ's followers and representatives, we are in a position to receive certain spiritual rights and privileges that belong exclusively to believers. We have access to the fullness of Christ's unlimited and heavenly resources.

Fifth, those who are under siege in the host nation may seek and receive refuge in the embassy of another nation at the ambassador's directive or discretion. As believers, those who are in the world very often find refuge, help, or safety within our homes, including our extended church home. In a very practical way, we provide ministry to others in the form of resolving their very practical and life-threatening problems.

Sixth, those who seek to emigrate from a host nation very often file their first paperwork toward that end in the embassy located within their home nation. In other words, a person desiring to emigrate from Nation X to the United States often goes first to the U.S. embassy or consulate office located within Nation X.

As believers in Christ, our homes and churches are the primary places where those who are residents of the world find a means of transferring their official residency to heaven. Politically, ambassadors might speak of a transfer of citizenship. In the Church, we generally refer to this process as spiritual conversion.

Seventh, much of what an ambassador does in a foreign nation is by example. Our United States ambassadors provide an American viewpoint, an American voice, an American presence to citizens of their host nation. They sometimes teach or explain why Americans do things in certain ways, or what Americans hold to be the principles undergirding freedom and democracy. Sometimes an ambassador's role is strictly ceremonial. The ambassador's mere presence signals that Americans welcome and desire an affiliation with others.

As believers in Christ and ambassadors of heaven, our foremost role in the world is to live our lives according to God's laws. Some of what we do is overt—teaching, explaining, proclaiming truth. Sometimes we play only a ceremonial role.

Eighth, ambassadors are periodically asked to make statements. Sometimes these are public speeches to large or small groups. Sometimes these statements happen casually over a dinner table or at a reception of some kind. Sometimes they are highly formal and serious statements made behind closed doors. The ambassador and other representatives of a nation deliver a message, perhaps even an ultimatum, to a foreign leader or influential person about something that the ambassador's nation believes should happen. These messages are nearly always intended to bring good to the people of the host nation and to the host nation's leader. The message may be one that is designed to avoid warfare or to avert disaster; but more likely it is an offer to help or to assist in a crisis situation.

As ambassadors for Christ, we are often asked to make statements for Christ. Most of these happen within the flow of our lives. We speak to those we meet in supermarkets, the corporate cafeteria, the club house, or the fitness center. Sometimes the Lord directs us to make formal presentations or to give a specific message to another person.

Ninth, an ambassador almost always speaks at the request of the host nation. The people in the host nation have questions, want information, or seek advice. Only on rare occasions does an ambassador take the initiative to speak outside his embassy. This, too, is the pattern for God's people. We very often speak about Christ and about our heavenly homeland when we are asked or invited by others to speak. There's something about our being Christians that intrigues people. There's something about what we believe that they want to know. There's something about our presence and our freedom in Christ that they desire to have in their own lives. Only occasionally does the Lord specifically direct us to take His message to a person, and the message we carry is virtually always to be for the ultimate good of the person to whom we take it.

Tenth, an embassy functions as a formal link between a host nation and a foreign land. When one does business at an embassy, he or she does so as if in another nation. The embassy is highly visible within the city where it is located, but its greater importance is unseen. The embassy is a genuine source of political power linking the two nations. Thus, it is a very serious gesture when a nation closes its embassy in another nation. That action almost always signals a serious breach between the two countries.

Our Christ-centered homes and churches are links between heaven and earth. They are the conduits through which heavenly transactions often occur. It is important that our personal embassies be visible so that others know where to turn in times of crisis or when they are in need of spiritual comfort or wisdom.

Women have the power to be Christ's ambassadors in the world. In summary, our job description as an ambassador is as follows:

1. We follow heaven's laws and protocol.
2. We take our orders from heaven. We look to the Lord to give us moral direction, commandments, and guidance.
3. When we are under attack, we request help first and foremost from heaven. We pray!
4. We enjoy special spiritual privileges as daughters of the High King of heaven.
5. We provide a place of refuge for those in need.
6. When others come our way seeking entrance into heaven, we help them make their decision for Christ. We pray with those the Lord sends to us so they might have eternal life and live with us forever as our neighbors in heaven.
7. We live as exemplary Christ-followers wherever we go, manifesting the principles of heaven in our behavior on earth.
8. We share the gospel with others in casual conversations, in formal presentations, and when invitations and opportunities present themselves.
9. We speak about Christ primarily when we are asked, and also when the Holy Spirit directly compels us to carry His Word to another person.
10. Our homes and churches are to become spiritual landmarks, bridging the power of heaven and the needs of the earth.

Some women fulfill the role of ambassador without stepping outside the boundaries of their own routines and obligations in the world. Other women are asked to speak outside the walls of their "embassy"—their home or their church.

One woman I know, Maggie, truly considers her home to be an outpost of heaven. She has designated one room in her home as a way station for evangelists and other Christians who are

passing through her city and are in need of shelter or just a dose
of rest and relaxation. The guest suite in her home is filled with
Christian literature, which she freely gives to those who come to
visit or who spend the night in her home.

Maggie spends time every day asking the Lord what it is
that He wants her to do, and she prays specifically for those who
will come to her doorstep. It's no mystery that strangers often
come knocking. Maggie is a living example of what another friend
has taught me about fulfilling God's will in her life: "You only
have to answer your phone, answer your door, and answer your
mail. God knows where you live, and He will send people to
you."

Maggie's home is a place of refuge. Many a friend has come
to Maggie's home to seek advice, cry on her shoulder, or pour
out a heartfelt concern for her to pray about. Maggie has her
coffee pot on from eight o'clock in the morning till noon, and a
tea kettle bubbling from two o'clock till four o'clock every afternoon. She's always ready for company.

Now, Maggie doesn't teach a Sunday school class, conduct
seminars, or lead a woman's organization. She attends church
and a Bible study regularly, but she is not a formal leader in
either. Still, she is very active as a Christian ambassador. Her
primary embassy is her home.

Some of those who come to Maggie's house seek a personal
relationship with Christ Jesus. Maggie prays with them to experience the Lord's forgiveness and empowerment by the Holy Spirit
to live a life pleasing to God. Others have specific questions about
their walk with the Lord. Maggie answers them as best she can.

How do these people know to come to Maggie? Other people
send them to her. The clerks at the local market, the cosmetolo-
gists at the nearby beauty salon, and the secretary in her church's
office all know that Maggie has a warm heart, a listening ear, and
a strong faith. And of course, those whom she has helped are
quick to recommend Maggie as a source of spiritual wisdom and

love. Maggie doesn't solicit people to help. She simply makes herself available.

When her church needs someone to host a visiting minister, missionary, or member of a traveling youth or music group, Maggie is called and she always provides a warm welcome, a comfortable bed, hearty meals, and time for rest and renewal.

Is Maggie a minister? Absolutely.

Is she an ambassador for Christ? Most definitely.

Is her home an embassy of heaven? It certainly is.

Maggie is doing something almost every Christian woman finds natural and feels capable of doing.

....
Bible Metaphors for Witnessing

The Bible has four great metaphors for being a witness. Each of them embodies a concept that is vital for our lives. As a whole, these metaphors give us a functional working definition for our jobs as ambassadors.

Fountains

The first metaphor is that of a fountain. The prophets foretold of Christ using this metaphor. Joel 3:18 says that a "fountain shall flow from the house of the LORD"—a fountain that would water the valley of acacia trees. Acacia wood, which is also called shittim wood, was used in the tabernacle, for the woodwork of the Ark of the Covenant, and for the altars and their staves, the table, the boards, the bars, and the pillars. In other words, Christ's Spirit would flow to nourish those who dwell within God's Holy Place and who will be vessels of His Holy presence.

The prophet Zechariah said that "a fountain shall be opened for the house of David and for the inhabitants of Jerusalem, for sin and for uncleanness" (Zech. 13:1). Heaven has a river of life. The Holy Spirit is likened to a river of living water. Jesus taught, "He who believes in Me, as the Scripture has said, out of his heart will flow rivers of living water" (John 7:38).

This idea of living waters and fountains is that of a bubbling artesian well, a source of fresh water that continually gurgles forth from a wellspring that often breaks through from rocky crevices deep in the earth. Fountains such as these create oases in deserts. As underground sources of water, they feed the cisterns and wells that are mentioned in the Bible. They are always associated with purity, freshness, cleansing, and life.

Christ is our fountain. His Spirit inside us causes us to become fountains to others. Our purpose as fountains is to continually bring forth praise to the Lord and to become nourishing sources of life to others, helping to meet their physical and material needs, as well as their emotional and spiritual needs by pointing them to the true Fountain, Christ our Lord.

As ambassadors, we are called to "bubble over" with Christ's presence. People who are in need of refreshment will come our way when we do.

Do people respond to others who manifest joy? Always. We intuitively are drawn to others who give to us, who refresh us, who encourage us, who are people of spontaneous joy and praise. We seek out those kinds of friends. We love being around people who have an infectious love of life.

We are commanded in the Scriptures to *rejoice*. In other words, we are commanded to be women of joy. Yes, it's a commandment. We are told to rejoice, and again the Scriptures say, rejoice. Joy is to be our hallmark, our reputation.

When we have this joy flowing from us, others will come to drink. We won't have to seek them out or even invite them our way. They'll come. We need only to make sure that our embassies remain accessible to them, and that we have an open-door, open-heart policy toward those who come to drink from our spiritual wellsprings.

Salt

Jesus said to those who followed Him, "You are the salt of the earth; but if the salt loses its flavor, how shall it be seasoned? It is then good for nothing but to be thrown out and trampled underfoot by men" (Matt. 5:13). In Mark 9:50, this teaching of Jesus is phrased this way: "Have salt in yourselves, and have peace with one another."

Have you ever seen a salt lick in a pasture? That's our job in the world! We are to make the world thirsty for the One who alone gives living water, and who said about Himself, "Whoever drinks of the water that I shall give him will never thirst. But the water that I shall give him will become in him a fountain of water springing up into everlasting life" (John 4:14).

We are to have flavor and zest in what we say to others about Christ. Our words are to cause others to want to know Him. Our perfectly seasoned words are to be enticing, mouthwatering, and when subjected to the heat of the moment, our words are to give off an aroma that is to be a sweet-smelling savor to the Lord. In this way, we speak salty words, and yet live in peace with others.

Our words are not to jangle the nerves or be abrasive. They are not to alienate or condemn. Rather, they are to challenge, inspire, provoke thought, and compel positive action.

Salt in ancient times was a precious commodity. It was used for purification, preservation, and healing purposes. Our words and deeds are to convey these same principles. They must purify the world, preserve what is holy and good, and bring healing to wounded lives.

Leaven

Leaven is used as a metaphor in two ways in the New Testament. Jesus used leaven to describe the action of the self-righteous religious leaders of the day, who had infected the population of God's people with false teaching and acrimony. Jesus warned against this type of leaven.

Part of the Passover celebration includes eating unleavened bread and ridding a house completely of all leavening agents. Paul wrote to both the Corinthian and Galatian churches that they should be aware of false teachings and sin that can act as leaven in the midst of the body of Christ. Paul told the Corinthians to "purge out the old leaven" and become new lumps of unleavened dough, "for indeed Christ, our Passover, was sacrificed for us." (See 1 Cor. 5:7.)

This same principle of leavening, however, can be used for good. Jesus used leaven to describe the witness of godly people, teaching that the kingdom of God "is like leaven, which a woman took and hid in three measures of meal till it was all leavened" (Luke 13:21).

We as God's women are to have a "rising" influence upon the whole world. We are to help our culture as a whole rise to a new level of excellence, achieve and maintain a higher moral standard, and rise up in faith.

How does yeast work? In the first place, yeast is only a small fraction of the ingredients in any loaf of broad. A very little amount can cause an entire loaf of bread to rise. It doesn't take very many women working together to bring about a great change!

Second, yeast is only good as long as it is active. If we pour out a package of yeast on a breadboard, we can almost see it jump and move. Yeast is alive. As Christ's women we are to engage ourselves actively in our various spheres of influence. We are to get involved and do so with a lively, energetic, and engaging attitude.

Third, yeast must be thoroughly mixed into the other ingredients so the entire loaf will rise evenly. We must be careful in our world not to form exclusive cliques, but rather to spread our influence throughout our entire culture, getting involved wherever the Lord leads us and refusing to become exclusive in any of our actions or memberships.

Yeast is triggered into action when it comes into contact with liquid. Yeast mixed in dry flour has absolutely no effect upon it. But add a little water to that flour, and watch the yeast go to work. Water throughout the Scriptures is a symbol of Christ's presence. Again, we come back to the fountain. As Christ's leaven in this world, we have our greatest influence when we are totally in line with the purposes and plan of the Holy Spirit. We must at all times seek out the direction that the Holy Spirit is taking within a particular group of people, asking ourselves continually, "What is God doing here and how can I best be used by Him? What is God's purpose and plan right now, and how can I be His active agent in the midst?"

So often we make our plans and then invite God to be part of them. Instead, we need to find out what God has planned and then ask Him how we might be involved! Our being yeast is to no effect unless we are united with Him in purpose and function.

Once bread has risen and been baked, the yeast cannot be discerned other than by its rising effect and the taste it gives to bread. It cannot be picked out like raisins or nuts. It cannot be seen. As yeast bread bakes, it gives off a wonderful aroma. Bakeries often entice buyers by allowing the aroma from their ovens to permeate the surrounding neighborhood or shopping area. Yeast adds flavor and texture. These are our roles as Christ's handmaidens. We give off an aroma that draws others to Christ. We add flavor to Christ's body. We bring a texture of lightness, not heaviness—an atmosphere of welcome, not of gloom.

Light

Perhaps the foremost metaphor for God's people is that they are to be light. Jesus said of Himself, "I am the light of the world. He who follows Me shall not walk in darkness, but have the light of life" (John 8:12).

He said about us, "You are the light of the world. A city that is set on a hill cannot be hidden. Nor do they light a lamp and put it under a basket, but on a lampstand, and it gives light to all who are in the house" (Matt. 5:14–15).

Lamps in Bible times were oil lamps. Wicks rested in clay containers filled with oil. These wicks often were made of tightly twisted scraps of old garments, what we would call rags. The Scriptures refer to our sin as filthy rags.

Oil in the Scriptures is a symbol of the Holy Spirit. It is the sin in our lives that the Holy Spirit promises to burn from our souls, cleansing us in the process and causing us to become a witness to others in the process.

As those in the world see us freed from the bondage of sin and living transformed lives, they become curious about us. We often hear nonbelievers say about believers, "There's something different about that person," or, "I can't put my finger on it, but he's changed," or, "She seems so joyful all the time." People comment innocently but openly about how the faces of Christians seem to glow. All of these expressions reflect an awareness on the part of the unredeemed world that something positive and good is happening or has happened to a person. What these people truly are responding to is the work of the Holy Spirit in freeing a person from guilt and sin.

We don't light ourselves. The finger of God lights our lives just as He did for those who received the manifestation of the Holy Spirit at Pentecost after Jesus ascended into heaven. (See Acts 2:4.)

What is the true nature of the light that glows from our clay vessels, our earthen bodies? It is the light of love. The Scriptures teach us that the Holy Spirit writes the law of love upon our hearts. It is our love that lights up the world and drives away darkness, not our words, not our personal appearance, but our loving actions! First John 2:10–11 says, "He who loves his brother abides in the light, and there is no cause for stumbling in him. But he who hates his brother is in darkness and walks in darkness, and does not know where he is going, because the darkness has blinded his eyes."

In summary, as Christ's ambassadors, we are to bubble with joy. We are to speak zesty, salty words that cause others to want to know Christ in a deeper and ever more intimate way. We are to rid ourselves of evil influence, both as individuals and as bodies of believers. We are to become leavening agents in our world, working in tandem with Christ to raise the standard of His kingdom. In the process, we are to infiltrate every aspect of the world's systems with His love, and to actively engage ourselves with others so that they will be drawn to Christ until they experience with Him the most intimate spiritual relationship possible.

We are to allow the Holy Spirit to burn sin away from our lives and leave us pure and glowing vessels of love, always seeking ways in which we can love others and meet their needs.

A woman has the power to be a fountain, a salt shaker, a packet of yeast, and a lamp in her world. Every woman can do this as Christ's witness in the world!

The Great Witness of Bible Women

The Bible has a number of examples of women who were witnesses for the Lord in the ways that have been described.

Huldah was sitting at home one day when five men came to her for spiritual counsel. These men had found scrolls of the Law while repairing the house of the Lord. When the scrolls were read to the king, he tore his clothes in anguish because he realized the people had not been obeying the commandments of God. He sent the priest, a scribe, a servant, and two other men to Huldah, who had a reputation as a godly woman and a prophetess.

A prophetess is a woman who is filled with God's Holy Spirit and speaks the truth that God imparts to her. Sometimes that truth involves future events, or the foretelling of the consequences that a current evil trend will yield. Sometimes that truth is the proclamation of the gospel of Jesus Christ. Sometimes it is a word specific to a particular people, time, and situation. Sometimes it is a word that is universal and related to the perfection of God's commandments and purposes.

Huldah had a reputation for speaking God's truth.

The account of Huldah's encounter with these five men is recorded in 2 Kings 22:14–20.

> So Hilkiah the priest, Ahikam, Achbor, Shaphan, and Asaiah went to Huldah the prophetess, the wife of Shallum the son of Tikvah, the son of Harhas, keeper of the wardrobe. (She dwelt in Jerusalem in the Second Quarter.) And they spoke with her. Then she said to them, "Thus says the LORD God of Israel, 'Tell the man who sent you to Me, "Thus says the LORD: 'Behold, I will bring calamity on this place and on its inhabitants—all the words of the book which the king of Judah has read—because they have forsaken Me and burned incense to other gods, that they might provoke Me to anger with all the works of their hands. Therefore My wrath shall be aroused against this place and shall not be quenched.'"' But as for the king of Judah, who sent you to inquire of the LORD, in this manner you shall speak to him, 'Thus says the LORD God of Israel: "Concerning the words which you have heard—because your heart was tender, and you humbled yourself before the LORD when you heard what I spoke against this place and against its inhabitants, that they would become a desolation and a curse, and you tore your clothes and wept before Me, I also have heard you," says the LORD. Surely, therefore, I will gather you to your fathers, and you shall be gathered to your grave in peace; and your eyes shall not see all the calamity which I will bring on this place."'"

The men who went to see Huldah took this word back to the king. Hers was a bad news, good news prophecy. For the people of the land the message was this: "You have sinned and you will suffer the consequences." The message to the king was, "You have humbled yourself before Me and as long as you live, you will not see the punishment God is going to bring upon those who have sinned."

The king recognized Huldah's prophecy as truth and he acted on her words. He did not in the least dismiss her words by saying, "Well, that's one woman's opinion" or "Why did we ask a woman?" Josiah the king didn't send men to Huldah because she was a woman, but because she was a prophetess, a person filled with God's Spirit and speaking God's truth.

Josiah made a covenant with the Lord to follow the Lord's commandments, and He ordered that all false idols and objects used in Baal worship be taken from the temple of the Lord and burned. He removed the idolatrous priests, and cleansed the land of idol worship and evil religious practices, including ridding the land of all those who consulted mediums and spiritists. Finally, he commanded the people to keep the Passover as it was written in the book of the covenant.

The writers of the Bible say this about King Josiah: "Before him there was no king like him, who turned to the LORD with all his heart, with all his soul, and with all his might, according to all the Law of Moses; nor after him did any arise like him" (2 Kings 23:25).

Huldah never had to leave her home to give a powerful witness to a king. We have no indication that she ever met the king face to face. Still, her prophecy related to the unearthed scrolls of the Law caused a phenomenal change in her land and a massive return of the people to following God's commandments.

I recently met a woman named Elizabeth who functions as a prophetess from her home. How so? Elizabeth writes letters. Some are to political leaders. Some are to religious leaders. Still others are to people whom she reads about in her newspaper or hears about from friends—generally speaking, these are people facing crises.

Elizabeth spends an hour before breakfast in prayer, asking the Lord to direct her letter writing of the day. After breakfast, and while still at her breakfast table overlooking her garden, she pulls out her best stationery and spends two hours handwriting letters of truth and encouragement. She encourages those to whom she writes to keep their faith in God, to have boldness in making right decisions, to open themselves up to receiving love from others. Her letters are warm, loving, and a blessing. She doesn't condemn. She doesn't give advice on particular issues. In the process of writing, however, she does state what she is thankful for, especially her blessings of freedom, health, and life itself.

Elizabeth is ninety-two years old. She writes truth to others. And she does it in a way that is salty, yet refreshing—convicting, yet heartwarming. She writes with love.

························

Being a Witness in Your Daily Routine

Mary Magdalene and several other women were going about a customary ritual when the Lord called them to be His witnesses in a unique and wonderful way.

They were headed to the tomb where Jesus had been taken so that they might add spices to His body, a practice that allowed a corpse to decay without offensive odor. The more spices wound in the grave clothes of a corpse, the more generous the act of love being expressed to that person. Mary and the other women went as a group to express their love for their Lord in a very practical way.

When they got there they found grave clothes, but no body. Jesus had risen from the tomb, and when Mary Magdalene saw Him in the predawn light and through the blur of her tears, she didn't recognize Him. She assumed He was a gardener. It was only when He called her name that she recognized Him and rushed to cling to Him. Jesus didn't allow her to hold Him back in any way. Rather, He sent Mary on a witnessing mission. He said to her, "Go to My brethren and say to them, 'I am ascending

to My Father and your Father, and to My God and your God.'"
(See John 20:1–18.)

The account of this story in the gospel of Matthew tells us
that Jesus also sent this message by Mary: "Do not be afraid. Go
and tell My brethren to go to Galilee, and there they will see
Me" (Matt. 28:10).

Mary Magdalene immediately went and told the disciples
that she had seen the Lord and gave them the words He had
spoken to her.

The disciples were not as smart as Josiah. They didn't believe what Mary Magdalene said (see Mark 16:11). Eventually,
however, Peter and John went to the empty tomb.

When Jesus appeared to the disciples later that night, He
rebuked their unbelief and hardness of heart because they did
not believe those who had seen Him after He had risen. Jesus
expected His disciples to listen to the words He had given a
woman to speak!

Mary wasn't seeking a message from Jesus. She wasn't looking for a platform in the midst of the disciples. She was going
about a customary, rather routine, and yet sacred ritual when the
Lord revealed Himself to her and gave her a message to tell.

We are told elsewhere in the Scriptures that Philip, one of
the first deacons in the Church, "had four virgin daughters who
prophesied" (Acts 21:9). Each of these women was asked to be
a witness for the Lord, and also to give a witness for Him as they
were asked, as the Lord commanded them, or as the Holy Spirit
directed them.

As a Christian woman your first and foremost concern in
being a witness is to line up the activities and actions of your life
so that you are obeying God. Your first and foremost concern in
giving a witness about Christ must be to speak only the words
that He has asked you to speak.

. . . .

Should Women Give Witness in Church?

One passage of Scripture has been cited frequently to silence women in the Church. It is 1 Timothy 2:11–15:

> Let a woman learn in silence with all submission. And I do not permit a woman to teach or to have authority over a man, but to be in silence. For Adam was formed first, then Eve. And Adam was not deceived, but the woman being deceived, fell into transgression. Nevertheless she will be saved in childbearing if they continue in faith, love, and holiness, with self-control.

Women and men were segregated during worship services of this period, a practice stemming from the synagogue. This practice continues to this day in orthodox synagogues. In one particular synagogue I visited in Jerusalem, I found myself in a balcony filled with women. Below, the men carried out the ritual of the prayers and the reading of the Law. All around me, women were chattering with their friends and talking to their children. They were discussing what they had prepared for the Sabbath meal and were generally catching up on the activities of the past week. The balcony was pretty much abuzz with loud whispers and hushed voices. They apparently didn't think the men below could hear them or that they were to participate in any way with the general ritual of the service.

On the front row of the balcony, several feet away from all the other women, was a woman who was leaning over the edge of the railing, in earnest desire to hear all that was going on below. She seemed to be hanging on every word she heard, and I could see her mouth moving in silent participation as the prayers were spoken.

I think of that woman every time I read the admonition Paul gave to Timothy, "Let a woman learn in silence with all submission." The submission is not to men or to the ritual, but to the Lord. The key fact is that Paul wanted women to *learn* what was going on! Elsewhere, women were prohibited from learning, or they were certainly not encouraged to learn. Paul wanted the women in the church that Timothy led to be fully informed and to learn every aspect of the gospel.

Timothy was left in charge of the church at Ephesus. Paul had taught there for two wonderful years filled with great miracles and powerful spiritual conviction and renewal among the people, including a massive burning of evil fetishes and magic books.

The hill above the city of Ephesus was dominated by a huge and magnificent temple built to the goddess Diana. The religion of the city was goddess religion, and specifically, worship of Diana, goddess of fertility. Any person who had grown up in the culture of Ephesus had been subjected to this influence.

Apparently, some of the goddess worship had crept into the Christian church. One of the twisted and warped teachings of Diana worship was this: Because men were born from the bodies of women, women were more important than men. Thus, women had natural authority over men. They also cited the fact that men nursed from women's breasts. Boys listened to their mothers' commandments. Goddess worship taught (and still teaches today) that women should be in charge. As evidence for this claim, the pagan women of Ephesus pointed toward the wisdom, magnificence, and wonder of Diana, who epitomized the authority of women.

Some people at that time in history understood that a man impregnated a woman and was the father of a baby, but actually, that teaching was not widespread. Sexual practice was seen as the means of a woman fulfilling the uncontrolled lust of a man and thus, exerting a kind of power over him. In essence, men needed women for sex and by giving or withholding sex from men, women were in control. To the follower of the God of Abraham, Isaac, and Jacob, the birth of a child was seen as a gift from the Lord. The birth of a child to a pagan woman in Ephesus was regarded as a gift from the gods. Men weren't perceived as helping to create life in a woman's womb. And the blessing of a child was regarded as belonging to the woman.

Paul's statement to Timothy has much more meaning in the light of all that was taught and believed in pagan Ephesus. Paul reminded Timothy that according to the teachings of God's Word, woman originally came from man—not vice versa as Diana worship claimed. He stated that women were not to teach that women should have authority over men, as Diana devotees claimed. (The newest translations from the Greek give this interpretation: "I do not permit woman to teach authority over man.")

Paul stated that womankind was, indeed, saved through childbirth, referring to Eve's giving birth to a son whose line eventually included Jesus. (See Luke 3:23–38 for this genealogy.) And thus, because of Christ, women can know the fullness of God's salvation and redemption if they continue in faith, love, holiness, and self-control.

Diana worship involved cultic prostitution. Hundreds of women sexually entertained thousands of men every night in the temple of Diana in Ephesus as a part of goddess worship rituals. Paul's teaching stands directly against this, stating that women are not saved by having sexual relations with men, but rather, by having a spiritual relationship to Jesus marked by faith and love, as opposed to ritual and lust. The mark of a woman's salvation is to be genuine holiness. Women are to set themselves apart for God's service, not make themselves prostitutes for men. A woman is to exercise her faith, love, and holiness with self-control.

Paul didn't want women to remain ignorant. He wanted them to learn. In the early church, it was vitally important that unlearned, uneducated women not attempt to teach the nuances of Scripture. The same would hold for any unlearned person suddenly given a platform from which to teach. Great error could have resulted and spread like wildfire if this had been allowed in the early church. The church today also benefits most when those who teach are thoroughly familiar with all Scripture.

Paul wanted women to learn . . . and then to teach. This is evident in Titus 2:3–5, where Paul advises that older women should be "reverent in behavior, not slanderers, not given to much wine, teachers of good things . . . that the word of God may not be blasphemed." He specifically told older women teachers to teach young women to love their husbands and children, to be discreet, chaste, homemakers (which included great economic and moral responsibility), good (in spiritual character), and obedient to their husbands. This same Paul advised husbands to love their wives, provide for them, and take tender care of them.

The overriding teaching of Paul on this matter of women speaking in the church is not a put-down, as has been so often claimed. Rather, it is a teaching of exaltation. Women were to learn the things of God, and then teach those things to others. That was not the case in Judaism. His teachings, at the same time, were strongly in opposition to goddess worship.

Paul was forging a new role for women. In his letters, Paul's warm greetings to women are evidence that he considered them to be colleagues in the faith.

....

A Witness Through the Holy Spirit's Gifts

Finally, women in the early church were expected to minister to others "as the Holy Spirit gave utterance."

They spoke words of wisdom and knowledge. They gave words of faith. They were prophets of the truth of God.

Paul's teachings about the right and proper use of spiritual gifts, found in 1 Corinthians 12—14, are not limited to men. The central point he makes, however, is that all gifts are to be exercised in love.

Love is key. Spiritual oneness is the goal. Experience is always to be subjected to God's Word. All is to be done decently and in order.

As modern-day women, part of our role within the kingdom

of God is to speak timely and Holy Spirit-inspired words, but to do so with love, as a means of bringing people together, and with decorum. We are not to be led by our emotions, but to subject our emotions to the scrutiny of God's commandments. Obedience is required. Having a particular type of spiritual high or expressing emotion in a particular way is never commanded.

Again, think in terms of our embassies. An embassy is a place of beauty, civility, and peace—unless it is under siege or attacked from outside forces. When an ambassador is in residence, strong leadership ensures that the staff members cooperate and that the entire team pulls together.

As a Christian woman, you have the power to make sure that your home and your extended home—the local church building—are places where God's Word reigns supreme, where the gifts of the Spirit operate to pull a family together, where words of wisdom, knowledge, faith, and truth flow freely, and where all is done to bring about peace.

You have what it takes to be such an ambassador, and to exert authority over your own personal embassy—the outpost of heaven that the Lord has given you to occupy and from which the Lord of heaven will send you as His emissary to speak His words and be His representative.

The
Power to
Pray

Women can pray powerfully and effectively. In other words, women have the power to pray *and see their prayers answered.*

How many times have you heard someone say, "My mother always prays for me"? Countless people credit their mothers', aunts', and grandmothers' prayers for their spiritual salvation, healing of various kinds, and deliverance from evil. How many people do you know who have benefited from the prayers of women's intercessory prayer groups?

Even if you don't know a praying woman, you can become one. Hannah is the foremost biblical example of a woman who manifested the power of prayer.

Hannah was one of two wives of Elkanah. Each year Elkanah went to Shiloh to worship and sacrifice to the Lord. The two sons of the high priest Eli, Hophni and Phinehas, were priests to the Lord at Shiloh. Elkanah took his entire family with him when he went to Shiloh, and he gave portions of his offering to Hannah and his other wife, Peninnah, as well as to Peninnah's sons and daughters, so they might take part in the worship and sacrifice. To Hannah, Elkanah gave a double portion out of his great love for her.

Year by year, Hannah went to the house of the Lord, and

yet she bore no children. This grieved Hannah deeply. Not only did she have her own private agony over being barren, but Peninnah, not receiving the affection that Elkanah gave to Hannah but having borne children to him, repeatedly needled Hannah over her barrenness.

One year, this provocation from Peninnah was so intense that Hannah wept and would not eat while they were in Shiloh. Elkanah tried to comfort her, saying, "Hannah, why do you weep? Why do you not eat? And why is your heart grieved? Am I not better to you than ten sons?" (1 Sam. 1:8). But Hannah would not be comforted. She rose after dinner and went to the door of the tabernacle to pray.

Unknown to her, the high priest Eli had come to Shiloh and was sitting at the door of the tabernacle. He witnessed Hannah's tears and anguish as she prayed to the Lord. As part of her prayer, Hannah made a vow, saying, "O LORD of hosts, if You will indeed look on the affliction of Your maidservant and remember me, and not forget Your maidservant, but will give Your maidservant a male child, then I will give him to the LORD all the days of his life, and no razor shall come upon his head" (1 Sam. 1:11).

Hannah was so deeply troubled as she prayed that only her mouth moved. No sound came from her lips. As Eli watched her weep and mouth words and no doubt rock herself back and forth, he thought she was drunk. He said to her, "How long will you be drunk? Put your wine away from you!"

Hannah answered him, "No, my lord, I am a woman of sorrowful spirit. I have drunk neither wine nor intoxicating drink, but have poured out my soul before the LORD. Do not consider your maidservant a wicked woman, for out of the abundance of my complaint and grief I have spoken until now" (1 Sam. 1:15–16).

Eli told Hannah to go in peace, and that the God of Israel would grant her petition.

Hannah went back to the feast at that point and ate, her face no longer sad.

We have no indication in the Scriptures that anybody at the feast had missed Hannah during the time that she left and prayed to the Lord. Her husband and the others present no doubt thought that she left the meal, composed herself, and then returned in a happier frame of mind, willing at that point to eat and take part in the festivities. The next morning, Elkanah and his family arose and worshiped before the Lord, and then returned home.

The Scriptures say that "in the process of time" Hannah conceived and bore a son, and called his name Samuel. Samuel's name means "asked of the Lord."

For the next few years, Hannah stayed at home while the rest of the family went to Shiloh to worship the Lord. She told her husband she would not go with them until the child was weaned. Then she would take him, that he may appear before the Lord and remain there forever.

When Samuel was weaned, she took him to Shiloh and during that time of worship, she brought an offering of three bulls, one ephah of flour, and a skin of wine—a very generous offering for that time. After one of the bulls had been slaughtered, she brought her son to Eli and said, "O my lord! As your soul lives, my lord, I am the woman who stood by you here, praying to the LORD. For this child I prayed, and the LORD has granted me my petition which I asked of Him. Therefore I also have lent him to the LORD; as long as he lives he shall be lent to the Lord" (1 Sam. 1:26–28). She worshiped the Lord and prayed this beautiful and prophetic prayer:

> "My heart rejoices in the LORD;
> My horn is exalted in the LORD.
> I smile at my enemies,
> Because I rejoice in Your salvation.

No one is holy like the LORD,
For there is none besides You,
Nor is there any rock like our God.
Talk no more so very proudly;
Let no arrogance come from your mouth,
For the LORD is the God of knowledge;
And by Him actions are weighed.
The bows of the mighty men are broken,
And those who stumbled are girded with strength.
Those who were full have hired themselves out for bread,
And the hungry have ceased to hunger.
Even the barren has borne seven,
And she who has many children has become feeble.
The LORD kills and makes alive;
He brings down to the grave and brings up.
The LORD makes poor and makes rich;
He brings low and lifts up.
He raises the poor from the dust
And lifts the beggar from the ash heap,
To set them among princes
And make them inherit the throne of glory.
For the pillars of the earth are the LORD's,
And He has set the world upon them.
He will guard the feet of His saints,
But the wicked shall be silent in darkness.
For by strength no man shall prevail.
The adversaries of the LORD shall be broken in pieces;
From heaven He will thunder against them.
The LORD will judge the ends of the earth.
He will give strength to His king,
And exalt the horn of His anointed."

(1 Sam. 2:1–10)

The form of this prayer is not unlike a song. It may very well be the song that Hannah sang to her son, Samuel, while he was in the womb. In Bible times, pregnant women were encouraged to spend the first three or four months of their pregnancy in quiet and rest. They were not required to engage in their normal work and duties, but rather, were expected to use this time to prepare themselves for motherhood and to bond with the child in their womb. During these months, the mother was expected to participate in the spiritual formation of her child. The general thinking was that a mother of peace, holy repose, and adequate rest would bear a child who was strong, fully formed physically and spiritually, and wholly committed to the Lord from the womb until the day the child died.

In doing what she could to form her child's spirit, a mother customarily made up a song in honor of her baby. This song was generally composed over the first few weeks of the pregnancy, although at times the songs were sung in full form almost as a prophetic utterance. Once composed the song was then sung repeatedly to the growing fetus until birth, and thereafter became the child's foremost lullaby. The tunes and words of these songs were unique to each child. The words embodied everything the mother knew intuitively about her child, including what she felt the Lord had revealed to her about her baby and herself as its mother.

Hannah's prayer is one of exceedingly great joy. She begins by saying or singing, "My heart rejoices in the Lord!" Her prayer continues as one of great praise. She recounts the goodness of the Lord, His strength, His ability to lift up the lowly, His wisdom in judgment.

Hannah knew that she had dedicated her firstborn son to the service of the Lord, and her song is one that depicts a Lord worthy to be served with all of one's life!

Not only was Hannah's prayer to conceive answered by the Lord, but also her prayer for Samuel. He became the high priest of his people and anointed the first two kings of Israel at the Lord's command.

Each year when Hannah went to Shiloh to worship and make sacrifice to the Lord, she brought a new linen robe for Samuel. And each year, Eli blessed Elkanah and Hannah. Hannah bore three more sons and two daughters!

....
Hallmarks of Prayer

Hannah's prayers have several characteristics worthy of consideration today for women who want to have power in prayer.

Pray from the Heart

Hannah prayed from the depths of her soul. She came to the Lord with a deep desire. Her prayer was no passing whim or rote recitation. Hannah prayed from her innermost being, and she gave voice and vocabulary to her greatest longing.

You can pray an emotional prayer without your request flowing from the deepest recesses of your being, but you cannot pray a prayer from the core of your soul without emotion. Hannah's emotion was so intense that she couldn't even vocalize her words. She "spoke" them nonetheless.

Pray According to God's Will

Children have always been considered a blessing of the Lord. They were especially regarded in Bible times as a sign of God's favor upon a person's life, an indication that God desired for their seed to extend to the next generation. Hannah was requesting God to favor her with a child. She did not doubt that her child would come from God, or that her child would be a blessing.

So often today, I meet women who aren't sure about their prayers. They hope God might honor them. In fact, they aren't even sure if the answer they desire is in keeping with God's will for them.

Unless you *know* that you are praying in the will of heaven, you may very well be asking something of God that is against His plan and purpose for your life or the life of another person. God has no reason to honor your prayer if it is opposed to His plan.

The more scriptural way to pray is: "Lord, this is my desire.

If this desire is also pleasing to You, then please grant me this. If I am praying in error, I trust You to answer me in the way that will keep me totally in line with Your plan for my life."

For nearly a year, a friend and I fasted and prayed on Fridays at noon for two people very dear to us. Both of us felt wounded in our hearts by the person for whom we were praying. Our prayers were for the offending person to be healed, for repentance and a change of heart and life in the person who had wounded us, and for restoration of the relationships we felt had been breached.

We covered in prayer everything we knew to cover—from the person's prenatal memories, to their physiological makeup, to the sins of their forefathers back four generations. We prayed that Scripture after Scripture might become a reality in each of their lives.

Our final prayer on Fridays was this: "Lord, have Your way."

Did God answer our prayers? Most certainly, but not exactly in the way we had expected. Neither of us has any idea as to whether the person for whom we had prayed has been helped in any way. The relationships were not restored, although we both have a deep and abiding sense of peace about these relationships. Our way was apparently not God's way!

The two people who benefited the most from these prayer sessions were my friend and I. God may or may not have healed the people for whom we were praying—indeed, that healing may still be in progress for them—but we do know with certainty that God healed us! He restored us to wholeness. He brought about a new awareness of the Scriptures in our hearts. The hurt we once felt we no longer feel.

Even as we ask the Lord to grant us specific requests, we must also give the Lord permission to edit our prayers so that they totally conform with what He desires to do. Rather than ask the Lord for permission to act in a certain way, we need to understand that He will act as He desires.

All of your prayers must be checked against the commandments in God's Word. God will not honor a petition that goes against the commandments He has already established. He will not grant a request to sin or to stray.

Pray in Obedience to the Lord

Hannah's desire was to serve God in all ways, including the bearing of righteous children. Her sacrifice was her son—to "lend" him to the Lord all his days, knowing full well that according to the Law of Moses, a firstborn son already "belonged" to the Lord. (See Exod. 13:15.)

People often attempt to barter with God. They don't want to follow His rules, but they do want His blessing. Therefore, they agree to do something they think God wants them to do in exchange for something they want. Hannah didn't barter with God. She made a vow to give Him back what was rightfully His!

Regardless of how God answers your prayers, you are to live in obedience to His commandments. God doesn't barter. He answers.

Those who come before His presence, according to the protocol of heaven, are those who come in the name of Jesus—those who believe in the sacrifice of the shed blood of Christ Jesus and who are regarded as heirs to all the riches and glory of the Father. You don't go before the King unless you know that you are His princess. He has no reason to extend the scepter of His mercy toward you or open up the coffers of His abundant riches—spiritual, emotional, physical, material—unless you come before Him with full and pure credentials. You pick up those credentials at the office of the Cross and nowhere else. You become God's princess when you confess your sins, receive His forgiveness, and seek to live according to His plan and commandments.

Pray with Boldness

Hannah walked right up to the door of the tabernacle to make her petition. This was the closest place on earth that she could go to experience the presence of God.

Many people shied away from the door of the tabernacle at Shiloh. The tabernacle was considered in its day to be the holiest place in all the land, and the people held it in such awe that even to draw near to the tabernacle required great courage. The prevailing thinking of the people was that if one came too close to God, and was the least bit impure, he or she would die.

Hannah knew she was in right standing with God . . . that her request was a righteous one . . . that the issue was a matter of great importance to her . . . and she appealed to God boldly.

Hannah was fulfilling every aspect of Psalm 37:3–6:

> Trust in the LORD, and do good;
> Dwell in the land, and feed on His faithfulness.
> Delight yourself also in the LORD,
> And He shall give you the desires of your heart.
> Commit your way to the LORD,
> Trust also in Him,
> And He shall bring it to pass.
> He shall bring forth your righteousness as the light,
> And your justice as the noonday.

When you know that you are praying within the will of heaven and that you are pure before God in making your petition, you have every reason to be bold. The Lord asks His people to "give Him no rest" in their petitioning. He desires that you come with courage into His throne room to make your requests known.

You have the authority as believers in Christ Jesus, and you have the ability. You are expected to manifest power in prayer.

I have a dear friend who prays with great boldness to the extent that I told her once that I didn't understand how she could feel so bold as to tell God what to do.

She replied, "I'm not telling Him what to do. I'm telling Him what I *want* Him to do. He knows the difference." And then she told me a story.

When she was a fairly young girl, her brother was struck by a car while he was playing in the street. She ran immediately to her father's study, where he was preparing his Sunday sermon. She said, "I had been told on numerous occasions not to interrupt my father while he was working on his sermon, but this time I knew he wouldn't mind. It never entered my mind to do anything other than rush into his study and cry, 'Dad, come help Brother!' " And then she added these words I've never forgotten, "There are some things I want my heavenly Father to do, just as much as I wanted my earthly father to help my injured brother."

How much do you desire your heavenly Father to act on your behalf? With that degree of desire, pray with boldness!

Don't Let Others Intimidate You

Hannah wasn't swayed by those who criticized her in prayer. When Eli the high priest called her a drunken woman, she spoke truth to him—she didn't run away and hide.

Don't let others intimidate you as you pray. God sees your heart. He knows your intent and your motive. Others don't, can't, and won't.

Acknowledge Answers to Prayer

Hannah didn't consider it luck or coincidence that she became pregnant. She said, "For this child I prayed, and the LORD has granted me my petition which I asked of Him" (1 Sam. 1:27).

Whenever your prayers are answered, and in whatever ways, you are wise to confess that the Lord has spoken and to abide by His answer and act upon it. You are wise to acknowledge all of your blessings as coming from the Lord, and not yourself. All thanksgiving, honor, and glory belong to Him.

Rejoice and Offer Praise in Prayer

Hannah was happy when she prayed, and she gave God praise and thanksgiving. Notice the attributes she speaks about the Lord:

He is *holy.* There is none like Him and no One else upon whom she can rely with such assurance. He is her Rock.

He is *omniscient.* He has all knowledge and all authority to judge.

He is *omnipotent.* No one can fight successfully against Him. It is entirely within His power to do what He pleases with His children, including the giving of children.

He is *immovable.* He is the foundation of the world. He is unshakable in His judgments. What God says, He does. What He does is absolute. Apart from the Psalms, this prayer of Hannah's perhaps represents the most complete survey of God's attributes found anywhere in the Scriptures. Hannah had a clear understanding of her Lord. An understanding like this only comes from a close and intimate relationship with the Lord, and Hannah had that.

Hannah's reason to praise God was personal and private. She wasn't voicing somebody else's praise. She was voicing her own.

The good news is that any woman can experience what Hannah experienced. You have the privilege to pray, to praise, and to live in right standing with your heavenly Father.

The Lord Empowers Women to Pray

At no time in the Scriptures do we find women precluded from the privilege of prayer. Nor do we find any example in which righteous women are denied answers to their prayers.

The holy service was reserved for men prior to the death of Christ on the cross, and yet even so, the court of the women was part of the temple design. Women brought sacrifices of their own to God throughout the Old Testament. They gave offerings of their own in the Temple during Jesus' time. (See Mark 12:42–44.)

After the Ascension of Jesus, the disciples returned to Jerusalem to do as the Lord had commanded—to wait in Jerusalem until they received the power of the Holy Spirit. The eleven apostles were in the Upper Room, where they continued with one accord in prayer and supplication "with the women and Mary the mother of Jesus, and with His brothers." Those who were empowered by the Holy Spirit to be Christ's witnesses in Jerusalem, Judea, Samaria, and to the end of the earth included women. Their prayers were answered when the day of Pentecost had fully come. (See Acts 1:8—2:4.)

When Peter was arrested and then miraculously led from prison by an angel, he went to "the house of Mary, the mother of John whose surname was Mark, where many were gathered together praying." (See Acts 12:5–19.) Women and men, meeting in the home of a woman, were praying around the clock for Peter's safety and release from prison. One of those in attendance that night was a girl named Rhoda. When Peter knocked at the door of the gate, Rhoda recognized his voice (a clear sign that she probably had been around Peter a great deal) and in her rush of gladness, she forgot to open the gate, and instead ran immediately to the group to tell them their prayers had been answered!

The church in Philippi began with a group of praying women. Paul came to Philippi, and on the Sabbath day he and his associates went out of the city to the riverside, "where prayer was customarily made." Paul and his missionary team sat down and spoke to the women who met there. The clear implication is that these women met regularly in this place for prayer. One of them was Lydia. Paul and his team were invited to her house to stay and the church took root in Lydia's home. When Paul wrote his letter to the Philippians, that letter no doubt was delivered to

Lydia's address. Paul refers to the Philippians as "my beloved and longed-for brethren, my joy and crown" (Phil. 4:1).

Oh yes, women have what it takes in prayer!

....

Using Prayer to Further the Kingdom of God

The Scriptures clearly teach that all growth in the kingdom of God begins with prayer. Prayer is the generator that brings heaven's will to earth. It is the most potent use of power at your disposal for extending the kingdom of heaven to earth.

This is not a book on prayer, but let me assure you of some facts about prayer.

You can pray at any time and in any physical position, circumstance, or situation. You may want to pray silently (as Hannah did) should that be more appropriate in a particular environment or with a particular group of people. Nonetheless, you can pray anywhere, at any time.

You can pray about anything. No problem is too small, no situation too mundane for prayer. Pain is pain, hurt is hurt, need is need. The Lord isn't too busy to hear any prayer.

You can pray in your own words. You don't need to voice your prayers in a Thee and Thou formal tone of voice. You don't have to read your prayers from a book, or have them administered, monitored, or mediated by someone else. As Hannah demonstrated, the most potent prayers come from deep within yourself.

You can pray alone or join your prayers with those of others. Hannah wasn't part of a prayer group. Lydia was. You can draw great strength from uniting your prayers with others. Jesus taught that if any two righteous people agree on a matter of prayer, it shall be done for them. (See Matt. 18:19.) Again, make certain that your prayers line up with the will of heaven.

If you need more information about prayer, many fine books and seminars are available. You should certainly take advantage of every opportunity you have to learn how to make your prayers more effective. This can be especially important if you are experiencing some type of block, or have hit a ceiling in prayer.

Keep in mind, however, that as much as you learn *about* prayer, this power will not be evidenced in your life until you actually *begin to pray!* There's no substitute for engaging in the real thing. And you can probably learn all that you need to know about prayer *as you pray.* Hannah didn't have a manual on prayer. She simply prayed.

The more you pray, the more you know how to pray. And the more you pray, the stronger you become in prayer. Prayer becomes easier. You become bolder. You find more and more of your prayers being answered. You sense the presence of God more as you pray. There's no substitute for time spent in prayer. There are no shortcuts in this area of spirituality.

Pray all types of prayer. Scripture says to give thanksgiving to God, to praise God, and to petition God. Thanksgiving relates to the blessings of God in our lives. Praise is verbalizing the many attributes and victories of God. Petitions are requests—the voicing of needs and desires. Christians are to give thanksgiving, praise, and make petitions for themselves and their families, churches, cities, and the nation.

Pray for all those in authority over you, for other believers, for peace, and specifically for the peace of Jerusalem.

Jesus gave His disciples a model prayer. (See Matt. 6:9–13 and Luke 11:2–4.) Other teachings by Jesus are also given with this prayer. Keep in mind that the Lord's Prayer is something of an abbreviation. Jesus, in typical rabbinical fashion, taught His disciples an outline for prayer. As you pray, for example, "Give us this day our daily bread," you should feel free to expand that line to include all of the needs you are facing in the day ahead. As you pray, "Our Father in heaven," let your spirit enlarge to encompass as many names and attributes as you can for your heavenly Father.

There's literally no end to your potential prayer list. But, you are probably wise to focus your prayers on specific things of the greatest urgency and concern to you. As you grow in prayer, branch out and extend yourself.

The Scriptures say to pray in all things and for all things. Whatever situation you face, you can pray for God's discernment and wisdom. You are to request what you need from God in any area of your life. You are to earnestly desire all that the Holy Spirit desires to give you, including the ability to pray in the Spirit. You are to be willing to pray for others whenever they come to you in need or you perceive that prayer is warranted on their behalf.

Finally, it is in prayer—in heartfelt and earnest expression to the Lord—that you begin to discern what power the Lord desires for you to manifest in any particular situation. Does He desire for you to use the power of seduction, transaction, training, witness, or perseverance? When are you to act? What are you specifically to say and do? These answers come as you pray. Weigh the impressions you receive in prayer against God's Word. Listen for confirming witnesses from other believers in Christ Jesus, and walk in faith.

Prayer is the beginning of any other form of genuine and righteous power you express. The foremost hallmarks of your life as a Christian woman are faith and prayer—praying in faith and acting in faith after you have prayed.

You have the power of prayer at your disposal. Use it daily, as often as needed!

9

The
Power to
Persevere

Women have the power to stand . . . and stand . . . and stand. Women are resolute, courageous, and persevering to the end.

Think about Eve for a moment. The biblical account in Genesis states that she was made from bone. Eve was made of what was considered in ancient times to be the sturdiest, strongest structural material in the body.

Bones give strength and shape to the body. It is the backbone that allows a person to stand upright. Bones allow for mobility. Each bone of the body is designed to move in relationship to other bones and tissues, to work for flexibility and range of motion in a flexed position, and to allow for resistance in a locked position. Muscles add to the strength and mobility, but muscles and tendons are attached to bone. In our spiritual lives, we are to be flexible to a point and accommodate others. We are to move when the Lord directs us to move. We are to stand immovable in areas that involve God's absolutes.

Bone is not visible from outside the body, except as it provides general definition. In like manner, character gives expression to behavior, but it is an inner quality. True courage and fortitude—a true spirit of persevering—does not flaunt itself. It is quietly, solidly kept within.

Eve was fashioned specifically from a rib bone. The rib protects the heart and lungs, the vital organs. Ribs are flexible, allowing the lungs to expand and contract. Ribs provide balance to help us stand and walk. Creatures with only a backbone slither. Creatures with rib cages walk.

The spiritual analogies are abundant!

Women who persevere do so with strength, poise, flexibility, and mobility. The very character fiber of a woman is meant to be that of bone, an inner quality of enduring with graciousness to the very end.

....

How and Toward What Ends Shall Women Endure?

Against what and for what shall a righteous woman stand in the kingdom of God?

Stand Against Evil

Although Paul used a military analogy to describe the stance against evil, he addressed his letter to both men and women in Ephesus. The letter to the Ephesians is perhaps the most family oriented letter of Paul. He offers spiritual counsel to wives, husbands, children, and household servants. And then he concludes, "Finally, my brethren, be strong in the Lord and in the power of His might" (Eph. 6:10).

Paul tells how we are to stand:

Put on the whole armor of God, that you may be able to stand against the wiles of the devil. For we do not wrestle against flesh and blood, but against principalities, against powers, against the rulers of the darkness of this age, against spiritual hosts of wickedness in the heavenly places. Therefore take up the whole armor of God, that you may be able to withstand in the evil day, and having done all, to stand.

> Stand therefore, having girded your waist with truth, having put on the breastplate of righteousness, and having shod your feet with the preparation of the gospel of peace; above all, taking the shield of faith with which you will be able to quench all the fiery darts of the wicked one. And take the helmet of salvation, and the sword of the Spirit, which is the word of God; praying always with all prayer and supplication in the Spirit, being watchful to this end with all perseverance and supplication for all the saints—and for me, that utterance may be given to me, that I may open my mouth boldly to make known the mystery of the gospel, for which I am an ambassador in chains; that in it I may speak boldly, as I ought to speak. (Eph. 6:11–20)

Paul told the Ephesians that they were to be fully clothed on the inside with the character and provision of Christ Jesus. He just as easily could have described the everyday garments of a woman or a man, from girdle to hats and heels. Paul envisioned the stance against evil, however, as warfare. We are continually in a spiritual battle.

Women intuitively understand warfare even if they have never been on a battlefield, and even if they have never heard war stories told in smoke-filled back rooms. Warfare is the atmosphere in the air whenever someone attempts to hurt, destroy, or take over a person or other aspect of creation that a woman loves dearly. The day that a person strikes out against a woman's beloved spouse, child, or friend—look out. That is an evil day, a day in which war begins.

The battle dress that Paul described is primarily defensive. We are to draw our defensive strength of character from a knowledge of the truth, a keen and continual awareness of our spiritual salvation, and a firm assurance that we are in right standing with God (which is righteousness). We are to recall that we have prepared ourselves to spread the gospel of peace in this world, and that we have read, studied, memorized, and meditated upon the Word of God until it has become the very wellspring of all our thoughts and motivations. When the enemy slings lies, insults, and defamatory and inflammatory remarks our way, our faith rises up and says, "No, that isn't true about me or about the Lord."

Paul says that after we have done all, we are to stand in this strength of character against evil. Having done all means just what it says—that we have done everything we know to do or felt compelled by the Spirit of God to do. Standing in full armor is no cop-out for energetic confrontation of evil. It means that after we have exhausted all means of dealing with the crisis, problem, or need at hand, we stand in our relationship with the Lord.

We don't faint in weakness, lie down in surrender, give up and collapse, or sit and rest a spell. We stand firm on the inside— a signal to the enemy of our souls that we will not give in to him and will not give up in our pursuit of extending God's kingdom on the earth.

What do we do while standing strong? We pray. Very specifically, we pray in the Spirit. This term means different things to different people, but all denominations agree on one thing: we are to pray about a matter just as Jesus would pray. We pray as if our lips are His lips, our vocal cords are His vocal cords. One effective way to do this is to pray His words and put them into an active tense.

Do you have an edition of the Bible in which the words of Jesus have been printed in red ink or highlighted in some other way? Focus on those words. Turn them into prayers.

Jesus said, "Blessed are the peacemakers, for they shall be called [children] of God" (Matt. 5:9). We turn that into a prayer by saying to the Lord, "You alone, heavenly Father, are the Supreme Peacemaker. No one can turn a heart of rage and anger into a heart of peace except You. Help me to be Your peacemaker in this situation. Show me what to do and give me the courage to do it. I want Your blessing. I want to be known as Your child. Whatever I do, I want the result to be such that every person involved in this situation is fully restored to a peaceful relationship with You."

When Satan tempted Jesus, Jesus said, "Away with you, Satan! For it is written, 'You shall worship the LORD your God, and Him only you shall serve' " (Matt. 4:10). We turn that into a prayer by saying, "Lord, I've had it with Satan bothering me. I speak to him in Your Name, 'Get out of my life.' I declare once again before him and before You that I desire to worship only the Lord God, and to serve only You, Lord. Give me the strength to withstand this temptation and to follow what it is that You desire for me to say, do, and be."

We pray for ourselves, our loved ones, and as Paul said, "all the saints." We pray for those who are facing the onslaught of evil with us. In other words, when we find ourselves in a particular situation, we pray for all of God's people who are involved in it, not just ourselves. We pray for our leaders, that they may continue to speak boldly for Christ. We must remain steadfast in our prayers.

The image Paul painted may sound like being all dressed up with no place to fight. But that isn't at all the case. Elsewhere Paul taught that when we resist the devil, he must flee from us. In other words, the very sight of us being dressed in full armor and standing against evil in prayer is enough to cause the devil to stop the fight and leave. He may not go in the first five seconds of our stance. He may not go in the first five years! But, he will go. He must. We are the ones who don't budge one inch away from what we know to be true about Jesus Christ. Satan is the one who does the running.

In a very practical way, we say no to evil and then we refuse to compromise, change our minds, or give in.

If a colleague at work asks you to participate in an office plot to defame another person or take over another department, say "no."

If a neighbor wants to tell you the latest gossip about a mutual friend, say "no."

If your child requests permission to go someplace where you believe he or she will experience something potentially harmful to your child's soul, say "no." You need not give any reasons, make excuses for your position, or apologize for it. You can certainly explain to your child the reason for your position—why you believe that environment or those people have the potential to draw your child away from Christ's love. But, you may also be wise to say nothing. To criticize your child's friends may lead to your child defending them further. You have every right as a mother to say, "I don't believe this to be in your best interest." And let your word be final. As long as you are operating out of love and genuine concern for your child, are attempting to keep your child from evil, and are responsible for your child, you have the authority to make your word stick.

Is your political representative facing a vote on a law that you believe will contribute to the general moral decline of our society? Write or call your representative and say, "As one of your constituents, I say 'no' to this."

Don't make idle threats. If you give an ultimatum, be certain you are willing to follow through on it.

Don't take action without expressing your reason for doing so first. Otherwise, the person will react against your behavior and not your motivation. Tell a person "no" first, and then lock the door, get out of the car, refuse to go, take away the keys or toys, or do whatever else you feel is necessary to underscore your opinion.

My friend Carolyn said no to her sixteen-year-old child coming in after curfew. The established curfew of her home was midnight. When her son came home at 2:00 A.M., he found the door locked. She gave him one night of grace and informed him that the next time he came home late, she would not let him in the house. He tested her resolve.

Carolyn locked the door at midnight, and when her son came home at 3:00 A.M., she refused to give him entrance. He slept outside in his car that night. And he came home by midnight every night thereafter!

Jillian faced a worse situation. When she found marijuana in her fourteen-year-old daughter's room, she said "no." Her daughter said "yes." For a full year, they battled weekly about the daughter's drug use, with Jillian seeking out professional advice for both herself and her daughter. When her daughter continued to use drugs, Jillian intervened and admitted her to a hospital. Once her daughter had completed the program, Jillian put her into a private school noted for strict but fair and compassionate discipline. She visited her daughter at every opportunity, but continued to say no to her daughter's pleas to return home. Eighteen months after her daughter went to the school, she graduated from high school with honors and thanked her mother for saving her life.

Some call it tough love. Some call it a "just say no" campaign. The Bible calls it "standing in the evil day."

We are never to give in to evil, not even a little bit, or for even a brief period.

Stand Against Shame and Disgrace

Shame and disgrace are forms of evil, but the issues of shame and disgrace are so common and so subtle, that they are often overlooked as being evil.

Shame is anything we do to undermine the value and dignity of another person. It is an assault against a person's worth. Shame is when we say to another person, "You cannot be redeemed. You aren't worthy to stand in my presence."

Disgrace is a public expression of shame. It occurs any time a person says to a third party, "That person isn't worth anything." Prejudice, gossip, and bigotry are all manifestations of shame and disgrace.

Rizpah, a concubine of Saul, was a victim of shame and disgrace. She stood strong against it.

A three-year famine occurred in Israel and King David went to the Lord to ask what the cause of the famine might be. The Lord said, "It is because of Saul and his bloodthirsty house, because he killed the Gibeonites" (2 Sam. 21:1).

The Gibeonites were not part of the tribes of Israel, but a remnant of the Amonite people. However, the Gibeonites had come to the children of Israel at the time the Israelites had entered the Promised Land, and they had volunteered to serve the Israelites. The Israelites in turn had sworn to protect the Gibeonites. Saul had taken it upon himself to reverse this promise and had killed many of the Gibeonite people.

King David called a meeting with the Gibeonite leaders and asked them what would be required to resolve the breach of promise. The Gibeonites asked for seven of Saul's descendants to be delivered to them, so that they might hang them. King David agreed.

Two of the seven men that David sent to the Gibeonites were Armoni and Mephibosheth, the sons that Rizpah had borne to Saul. They and five others were hanged and left hanging as a sign to all the people that retribution had been made for the deeds of Saul.

There is only one verse in the Scriptures about Rizpah's response to the death of her sons, but it is a powerful expression of perseverance against shame and disgrace. Second Samuel 21:10 says, "Now Rizpah the daughter of Aiah took sackcloth and spread it for herself on the rock, from the beginning of harvest until the late rains poured on them from heaven. And she did not allow the birds of the air to rest on them by day nor the beasts of the field by night."

This scene is one of the most poignant and also one of the most gruesome in all the Bible. At the foot of the gallows where the bodies of her two sons and five other men were left hanging from ropes, Rizpah stood guard, night and day. She kept her vigil from the beginning of the harvest, in the late spring, until the time of the late rains, which is fall—a period of at least five months. During that time, she kept vultures and wild animals from tearing the flesh off the corpses. This, of course, was not a simple matter of "shooing away" little birds. Vultures are large birds and can be fierce, especially if they sense flesh easily available for the taking. The same is true for foxes, wolves, and other carnivorous animals. Rizpah's life may very well have been in danger on numerous occasions.

The Gibeonites left these bodies hanging from the gallows as a sign. But from Rizpah's point of view, this was a matter of great shame and disgrace. She could do nothing to stop the death of her sons, but she refused to allow their bodies to be disgraced by being ripped apart by scavenging birds and animals. Rizpah attempted to maintain honor for her sons.

In paintings of this scene, Rizpah is often portrayed as a wild woman with disheveled appearance, a mother driven mad by the death of her only two sons. It is just as likely, however, that Rizpah was a *determined* woman, forced by the task facing her to brave the elements. She refused to be comforted if it meant shame for herself or her family.

When the rains finally came, Rizpah was forced indoors, but by this time, the flesh of her sons' bodies no doubt was hardened and dehydrated by the sun into a leathery texture undesired by vultures and animals.

When King David was told what Rizpah had done, he gathered the bones of Saul and Jonathan, as well as the bones of these seven men, and he had them buried together in the family tomb in Zelah. David gave these men proper burial, one befitting a former king and his heirs.

In the end, Rizpah's action brought the results she desired—

an honorable burial for her sons and a position for them among Saul's family and heirs. She turned the tide of shame and disgrace by saying no to infamy with her one-woman vigil.

Stand for Good Until Good Is Accomplished

Two Bible women provide great examples of women who refused to be denied the good they desired. One of these women is fictitious, the heroine in a parable Jesus told about prayer.

> "There was in a certain city a judge who did not fear God nor regard man. Now there was a widow in that city; and she came to him, saying, 'Get justice for me from my adversary.' And he would not for a while; but afterward he said within himself, 'Though I do not fear God nor regard man, yet because this widow troubles me I will avenge her, lest by her continual coming she weary me.'
> . . . "Hear what the unjust judge said. And shall God not avenge His own elect who cry out day and night to Him, though He bears long with them? I tell you that He will avenge them speedily. Nevertheless, when the Son of Man comes, will He really find faith on the earth?" (Luke 18:2–8)

The woman demanded full retribution for a wrong committed against her. Jesus is not concerned in this story with what type of wrong it was, but rather He emphasizes her perseverance in demanding justice. She literally wore down and wore out this hardened, proud judge.

Sometimes we don't voice our perseverance with a firm "no," but with a continual, "please, please, please."

Each time this woman came to the judge to request an appeal, she had to come from a different angle in her argument, or with a new piece of evidence. That may be what women today have to do to get the justice due them. The point Jesus made is a strong one—this woman persisted until she got what she wanted.

The second example of a woman persisting for good is the story of a real woman who lived in what today would be Lebanon.

Jesus had traveled north with His disciples and when He reached the region of Tyre and Sidon, a woman came to Him. (See Mark 7:24–30.)

The Scriptures say that Jesus had entered a house in that area and "wanted no one to know it, but He could not be hidden." We don't know precisely how the woman heard about Jesus, but she managed to come to Jesus and she fell at His feet.

She was a Greek woman by culture, a Syro-Phoenician woman by birth, and the Gospel writer tells us that she "kept asking" Jesus to cast the demon out of her daughter. It is easy to imagine this scene—a woman bowed down at Jesus' feet, refusing to move, stating over and over, "Please cast the demon from my daughter, please cast the demon from my daughter."

We don't know with certainty all the particulars of this scene, but it is very likely that Jesus had entered a Jewish home in that region, as a righteous Jew would have been expected to do, and that this Greek woman came and fell at Jesus' feet while he was reclining "at table." At that time, meals were served on very low tables. Dinner guests often reclined on large pillows near the table, dipping pieces of bread into various sauces and dishes.

This woman may have been a servant in the home or a friend of one of their servants. If she was a servant in the home, she may have overheard some of the conversation going on at the table as Jesus taught or spoke about the kingdom of God, or as the disciples spoke of some of the great healing miracles among the Hebrew people in Israel.

If that is the scene, then the woman's actions and Jesus' words certainly make a great deal of sense. Jesus said to her, "Let the children be filled first, for it is not good to take the children's bread and throw it to the little dogs" (Mark 7:27). In essence, Jesus may have been saying, "Let Me share the good news of the kingdom of God with My host and his guests first."

Jesus used an example that would have been common in a dining setting. Small house dogs (some might call them lap dogs) were sometimes kept as pets. During meals, people customarily tossed their bones or undesirable scraps to the little house dogs. Jesus also was speaking within the culture of the Hebrews at that time when He referred to the Gentiles as little dogs. That was a common expression used by Jewish people for non-Hebrew people, but Jesus doesn't use the full force of the expression. Rather, He said "little dogs," those of the friendly, household variety.

Jesus was saying, "Let Me give the fullness of the gospel teaching to those in this home, rather than take the life-giving message intended for them—their bread—and toss it to someone desiring a scrap of a miracle."

The woman would not be dissuaded from her purpose. She persevered. She said, "Yes, Lord, yet even the little dogs under the table eat from the children's crumbs" (Mark 7:28). In other words, "If You have only a scrap of a miracle to give me, it's enough. I'll take the scrap. Little dogs get at least that much!"

Jesus agreed with her and told her that the demon had gone out of her daughter. And when the woman arrived at her home, she found the demon had indeed gone out from her daughter and her daughter was lying peacefully on her bed. Apparently a sickness was ravaging her daughter. Illnesses that caused convulsions, great fevers, or seizures were often thought to be demonic in nature. By the time this woman arrived at home, she found her daughter at rest, in recovery stage.

The woman refused to be insulted. She refused to be dismissed. She refused to slink quietly away. She persisted, and she got what she wanted from the Lord.

Not only did she say "please, please, please" in her attitude and actions, but she also said, "now, now, now."

....
Persevering in the Kingdom of God

The underlying motivation for persevering is never to be one of pride, hatred, revenge, or selfish desire. We certainly have the *power* to persist when we are motivated, but our use of power is not righteous unless our motive, goal, and methods are all righteous before God.

Our motivation for persevering must be firmly rooted in a love for others, a desire to see the weak receive justice, and a desire to see God's will accomplished.

A Love for Others

The Scriptures describe the nature of God's love toward His people as *chesed*—steadfast lovingkindness. This is love that cannot be swayed by circumstances or the other persons' behavior. We don't love a person because that person has sinned; we don't deny that he or she has erred. We love people *in spite of* their weaknesses, faults, sins, or errors. We persist in loving them in spite of what others say about them or do to them. We persist regardless of insults we may receive for taking our stance of love.

This type of love is the fervent love capable of covering a multitude of sins. (See 1 Pet. 4:8 and Prov. 10:12.) When we are motivated by this type of love, we find that our love persists. In many ways, we are able to persist because we love.

A Desire to See the Weak Receive Justice

The Scriptures speak repeatedly of the need to provide justice for the widows, orphans, and sojourners. In today's terms, these three groups of people would be abandoned women, abandoned children, and those without homes.

Justice is not merely fairness. It is full vindication. It is providing for a person's needs to the point where she or he is fully compensated for a loss, or fully helped to the point where the person no longer feels the ache of a loss. Justice requires a full resolution of the problem—a complete healing, a complete provision.

We have a right motivation for persisting when we stand and refuse to be moved until the person we encounter—whether a member of our family, a person who shows up on our doorstep, or a person about whom we hear—is helped to the point where the need in his or her life has been fully resolved.

Very often we limit the concept of justice to punishment of an offender. True justice for a victim involves meeting the need or resolving the problem of the offended.

A Desire to See God's Will Accomplished

Our motive of love comes from within, and this motive remains regardless of what another person does or how situations and circumstances may change. Our motive for justice comes from our encounter with needful people, and this motive remains until justice is complete.

This third type of motivation comes from the heavenly Father, and this motive remains until He lifts the burden from our heart or He proclaims the need no longer to be present.

We must be very certain that the thing we desire is in full keeping with the teachings of Jesus and the commandments in the Scriptures, and that it is not only for our own good, but also for the good of all other people. Cults easily fall into error and exclusivity when they claim that the teachings and commandments of the Scripture are being followed, but primarily for the good of themselves alone and the judgment of all others. The judgment of others is God's domain. God calls us to love and not to condemn or judge. (See Luke 6:37.)

We also must be very certain that it is God who is motivating us to action, and not simply a whim of the moment or a passing desire of our own.

How can we tell? First, we can subject what we perceive to be God's call to the test of time. Does this perception persist within us? Do other God-fearing people also have this perception over time?

Second, a true call from God grows over time. It does not diminish, but rather, it intensifies. Does the desire we have for good seem to burn within us as our destiny, to the point where we feel as if we must take action or we will be consumed by God's call?

Third, we must ask ourselves, "Does our call and desire bring glory to the name of Jesus, and blessing to His people? Or, is this something that will bring glory to me or to another person, and blessing to only a select few of God's people?"

Does it last? Does it grow? Does it bless others and glorify God? These are the three main questions to ask as we discern if something is truly a call to action from God.

We persist in love without end.

We persist for the cause of justice until justice is fulfilled.

We persist in our desire to see the will of God enacted, exacted, or accomplished until it is, and to God's satisfaction.

I once witnessed a woman named Allison persist until she received the good thing she desired.

Allison was active in a number of groups at her church, and eventually was chosen to be part of her church's board. Allison sat quietly through most meetings. When the time came for new business, she would quietly and graciously ask, "Is now the appropriate time to discuss what we are going to do as a church to help the street people?"

Allison was a member of a large downtown church. She saw homeless people every Sunday as she made her way into her church building, and over time, she came to recognize a number of the men and women, and they her. Allison saw the street people and had compassion upon them. She deeply desired to see something done to help them. She not only felt this was a good idea, but something that the Lord required of her and others in their church.

Meeting after meeting, month after month, Allison politely asked during the new business portion of various meetings, "Is now the appropriate time to discuss what we are going to do as a church to help the street people?"

At first, her question was dismissed with a wide variety of excuses about budgets, committees, organizational protocol, and so forth. Allison just smiled and persisted in asking. Some became upset with her for asking repeatedly. One man even insulted her in a meeting by saying, "No, Allison. That isn't new business. By now, thanks to you, it's old business!"

Allison just smiled and continued to ask. Eventually, something was done. And today, that church feeds breakfast to more than 250 street people daily, gives a sack of groceries to 40 needy families a week, and has an annual drive that makes new mufflers, knit caps, and gloves available to all who are in need of them.

Allison persisted until she saw the will of God enacted.

What Do We Do While Waiting?

Rarely do any of us get what we desire in a moment. We persist over time. What do we do while waiting, standing, persisting, persevering?

We pray. We pray for boldness, courage, wisdom, clear discernment, and an increase in our love. We verbalize and vocalize our petition to the Lord, just as the persistent widow described in Jesus' parable.

We continue to search the Scriptures. We search for additional information, promises, and commandments that are related to the situation in which we find ourselves, or the situation another person is experiencing. We ask the Lord to guide our reading of His Word and to reveal to us His insights and understanding.

We continue to state what we want, or what we don't want. We continue to voice our desires to God. We contact people who are in a position to help us in any way to achieve the goal we seek. This may be in the form of writing letters, calling people, sending telegrams or computerized messages, hosting teas, holding meetings, speaking to groups, engaging in conversations, or calling media talk programs.

We continue to hope. We continue to expect something good to happen to us, for us, in us, and through us. Hope is related to what we desire and to the most beneficial goal or result we can envision. We make our hope active in our lives when we prepare and plan for the day when we receive fully that which we are working toward.

We continue to have faith. We continue to believe that God is going to work all things together not only for our good, but also for the ultimate good of all people, and for the fulfillment of His plan. Our faith is placed in God and in His wisdom, not in our own desires. Hope is related to our desires. Our faith is related to God. We make our faith active when we give to others, trusting God to use what we give to supply their need and our own.

We continue to do what we know to do. That may be to do the work that God puts before us. It may be to pursue all avenues until they are exhausted. It may be to do nothing. Sometimes doing nothing is actually doing something! If we don't know what to do, or don't have any clear direction, we generally are better off doing nothing—other than to ask the Lord to reveal to us any actions we should take. We work, work, work, and rest when we no longer have the strength to work. As soon as we have regained strength, we work again.

In these ways, we exercise patience. Patience is an active quality, not a passive one. We choose to wait on the Lord. And we wait with open eyes and open hearts, eager to respond to the slightest prompting of the Holy Spirit.

....

Patience Is Active Waiting

Waiting is not sitting idly and watching the world pass by. Waiting is much more akin to that which butlers do in the presence of their employers. They wait in the wings, watching their employer's every move. When the employer signals, the butler responds.

Waiting is watching closely, anticipating eagerly, and then responding joyfully, effectively, and efficiently even before being asked.

When we say to another person, "Wait for me," we aren't giving the person a command to go to sleep. What we are implying is, "Stay here and watch for me to return."

Part of what we do in our persistence as Christian women is to watch—to look continually for what the Lord is doing, and to be on the alert for His presence and His mighty deeds in our midst. We wait on the Lord as His handmaidens, anticipating what it is that the Lord would desire for us to do for Him and on His behalf, and then to do that with such skill that we get the job done without His ever having to awaken us or order us to action.

James 1:4 says that we are to "let patience have its perfect work, that you may be perfect and complete, lacking nothing." When we persist in a godly manner, motivated by right desires, pursuing the right goals, and persisting in the right ways, our persistence produces something inside us. It gives us fortitude. It causes our faith to grow. It creates in us that elusive but fabulous thing called *character*. (See Rom. 5:3–4.)

We don't give up on the people who are important to us. And we don't give up on God. Jesus said that when we persist in our walk with the Lord, refusing to abandon our relationship with Him, we "possess our souls." (See Luke 21:19.)

....

Enduring to the End

Jesus said, "He who endures to the end will be saved" (Matt. 10:22). He said this after He had told His disciples that He was sending them out as "sheep in the midst of wolves." He told them to be harmless as doves and wise as serpents, to beware of the men who would deliver them up to councils or scourge them in the synagogue. He warned them about being brought before governors and kings to give testimony. He said that families would be torn apart because some in a family would believe His gospel and others wouldn't. And finally, He said that they would be hated for His name's sake.

Jesus expected His followers to outlast all of these problems and heartaches. Note closely what He told them, and through His Word, what He tells us:

We are sheep in the midst of wolves. We are subject to attack by and from others. The only hope that a sheep had of survival was to stay very close to its shepherd. If we are to survive in this world and endure to the end, we must stay close to our Shepherd.

We are to be harmless as doves and wise as serpents. Doves never attack another creature. Serpents are smart enough to slither into a rocky crevice when danger approaches. In persisting, we are never to verbally or physically assault others. When we sense danger approaching, we should run to the Rock of our salvation and hide there. (See Pss. 31:3; 62:2.)

We are to be wary of those who would persecute us. We are to watch out for persons or groups who would persecute us in our denominations and churches ("councils" and "synagogues"), or who would try to defame us publicly for their own political favor. Jesus didn't say we are to stop acting or speaking because of this persecution, but that we should be wary of it—in other words, skillfully sidestep as much persecution as possible.

Jesus also told His disciples that if they were called upon to give testimony, they would find the right words to say. They didn't need to prepare a speech in advance or worry about saying the wrong thing.

We are to stand against evil and for righteousness. We are called to do this, even if those we love the most disagree with us, threaten us, or abandon us. As painful as this may be to us, the alternative is even more painful. If we don't stand against evil or don't stand up for righteousness, we are going to have a dreadful twofold consequence. First, we will have an even bigger set of problems that will require an even stronger stance, which will likely cause more disagreement, stronger threats, or total abandonment. If we don't stem the tide of evil, the tide of evil will swamp us and capsize our lives. Second, and more important, by refusing to stand against evil or stand for good, we will be in middle-of-the-road danger. Lukewarm commitment and repeated compromise with evil cause us to lose favor with God—to the point where Jesus said in the Revelation of John: "I will vomit you out of My mouth" (Rev. 3:16).

We are to expect those in the world—those who are opposed to Christ Jesus and to God's commandments—to hate us. We can't expect them to like us, be friendly toward us, or approve of us. This does not mean that we have the privilege of hating them back. Quite the contrary! We are called to love them in return.

This also means that we should not seek to curry the favor of the unrighteous. They can't fully give us their favor and remain true to their evil natures or unrighteous ways. What we can expect is for them to make decisions that enable God's kingdom to expand and for believers to live in peace. Although evil people in authority over us may never give us their full approval, they can give us approval to behave in certain ways. A lawmaker, for example, may not like you because you are a Christian. That same lawmaker, however, may pass a law in your favor. Don't expect to be liked as you persist. Do expect to be effective, and to some degree, respected.

What was the mission on which Jesus was sending His disciples when He gave them these words of wise counsel? Jesus was sending His disciples out to preach this message: The kingdom of heaven is at hand. He was also sending them out to heal the sick, cleanse the outcasts (lepers), raise the dead, and cast out demons.

He said that if they would follow His directives as they

conducted their ministry of proclaiming the good news of God's kingdom, healing those who were sick, restoring the outcasts to full heavenly citizenship, raising those dead in sin, and casting out evil . . . they would be saved. In other words, they would come again into His presence. They would return to Jesus with a victory report.

We have the same mission as God's women today. As followers of Jesus, there's nothing in the Scriptures that precludes us as women from proclaiming the good news of salvation through Christ Jesus, praying for healing and wholeness in another person's life, restoring those who are outcast into full Christian fellowship, bringing a message of hope and life to another person, or requiring that evil flee from us.

If a woman persists in these aspects of active and loving ministry to others, and if she will stay close to her Shepherd, be wise in her behavior, be aware of potential persecutors, and expect *not* to be liked by all people, the promise of Jesus to her is that she will be with Him, and that He will be with her. She may not be rescued from all problems or all persecution, but she will experience an intimate closeness with the Lord. The woman who is tucked under the arm of Jesus is a woman who is truly saved—now and forever.

As a Christian woman, you have the power to persevere. Persist for the right causes, with the right motivation, and in the right ways. You *will* endure. You will know God's pleasure and presence.

You have what it takes to do this—all the way to the finish line!

10

....

Growing
in
Power

A little girl once explained her weight-lifting father's muscles to me in this way: "Big muscles come from big exercises with big weights."

How right she was, spiritually speaking as well as physically speaking!

Although most women probably do not aspire to have big muscles, most women do desire to become increasingly effective in whatever they undertake. They desire to get the job done. As smaller tasks are accomplished and needs are met, larger ones often loom in their place. The goal women must have is to grow in the ability to *apply* power. We have authority in the areas defined in this book. We have the latent skills necessary. As we apply our abilities and strength of character to meet needs, we will get stronger and even more powerful, and we will be better equipped to resolve bigger and bigger problems, meet bigger and bigger needs, and accomplish bigger and bigger goals.

Some people take vitamins, herbs, and minerals to become physically healthy. Some people take two weeks at a spa. Some people take their doctor's advice. In the spiritual realm, there are three things that a woman needs to "take" as she grows in her ability to apply power:

- Take a break.
- Take courage.
- Take action.

....

Taking a Break Doesn't Mean Quitting

Break time is not quitting time. Taking a break means to get alone, or to retreat with friends for the purpose of being apart from the world, and of sitting at the feet of Jesus.

There are two wonderful but very different examples of this in the Scriptures. Perhaps the better known is that of Mary, sister of Lazarus and Martha:

> Now it happened as they went that He entered a certain village; and a certain woman named Martha welcomed Him into her house. And she had a sister called Mary, who also sat at Jesus' feet and heard His word. But Martha was distracted with much serving, and she approached Him and said, "Lord, do You not care that my sister has left me to serve alone? Therefore tell her to help me."
> And Jesus answered and said to her, "Martha, Martha, you are worried and troubled about many things. But one thing is needed, and Mary has chosen that good part, which will not be taken away from her." (Luke 10:38–42)

Jesus wasn't criticizing Martha for working or for serving. He criticized her for allowing her work to distract her from His presence.

In like manner, Jesus isn't giving Mary license to be lazy. He no doubt expected her to have already helped in some ways, and to continue to serve again as needed after He had concluded what He was saying. If Jesus was willing to be flexible about mealtime and the manner of service, then Martha should have been flexible, too.

This wasn't a matter of some serve and some get waited upon. It was a matter of timing and priority. Martha had put meal preparation, her concept of service, above sitting at Jesus' feet and hearing His Word.

The central point of this incident is that we each must seek the presence of the Lord as the first priority in our lives. And for most of us busy women this means taking a break from our work.

A break to do what? Just to sit down and listen to what God might have to say. To spend unstructured and quiet time alone with the Lord. To pray and listen, to read His Word and reflect upon it, to pursue ideas that seem to spring from the Scriptures.

Mary probably knew the words of Psalm 27:4:

> One thing I have desired of the LORD,
> That will I seek:
> That I may dwell in the house of the LORD
> All the days of my life,
> To behold the beauty of the LORD,
> And to inquire in His temple.

Mary saw her home that day in Bethany as an embassy to which the Leader of her nation had come to visit. She was willing to drop all of her other duties to "dwell in His presence," even as He occupied her dwelling! She was content to sit at His feet, beholding His beauty, the masterful order and purpose and awesome creativity of His plan, and to ask Him questions and take His answers as being true in and for her life. In many ways, she made her living room that day a sanctuary for the Lord.

We grow in our ability to apply the power God has given us as we sit and soak up God's presence and His Word into the innermost core of our souls. Mary took a break, a time-out, to sit at Jesus' feet. We need to do likewise.

Another biblical example of taking a break is found in the Old Testament, although much of this particular type of break must be inferred.

Under the Law of Moses, women were considered unclean during their menstrual periods. The laws regarding this unclean state are described in detail in Leviticus 15. Essentially, a menstruating woman was to be "set apart seven days." Anyone who touched her or her bed or anything on which she sat was considered unclean. A man was not allowed to have sexual relations with an unclean woman; to do so meant the man was unclean for seven days.

If a woman's menstrual period lasted longer than seven days, she was considered impure all the days of her period.

On the eighth day, the woman was to bring two turtledoves or two young pigeons as a sacrifice, one as a sin offering and the other as a burnt offering, so that the priest might make atonement for her.

In a very practical way, this law prohibited a woman from sitting or lying down on anything other than the bare earth, or from touching the "clean" members of her family. As a matter of time and labor-saving efficiency, the custom developed that women went "outside the camp" during the time of their menstrual cycle. In essence, the unclean gathered together and took care of each other.

Many have stated through the years that this policy was a matter of hygiene and preventive health care. More recent research, however, clearly defines this practice as being spiritual in nature. A person was considered unclean if the person spilled blood or discharged bodily fluids of any kind. Life was equated with blood, so to spill blood was to diminish or take away an aspect or potential for life. In biological ways not known to the people of that age, the spilling of blood during a woman's menstrual period was, indeed, a sign that a cycle in which life might be procreated had come to an end.

The spilling of blood was considered a breach against the Life Giver, and thus, labeling this as sin and having a sin offering to bring the bleeding woman and the Life Giver back into "at-one-ment" were necessary.

Consider, however, the practicalities of women being together "outside the camp" for the entire duration of a menstrual period. In the first place, a woman was likely to be among friends. The more predictable and regular her monthly cycle and that of other women, the more likely she was going to see the same faces every month. Friendships were likely to develop across family lines. For a woman of that time, being outside the camp may very well be likened to a woman today attending a women's retreat.

What do women do today when they gather together? Invariably the conversation turns to family matters, romance and relationships, feelings, recipes, and various crises that the women have experienced or are experiencing. The same was undoubtedly true for women in biblical times. Women discussed their lives with one another. They shared tidbits of advice about what was working for them or joyful to them. They nurtured each other in their pain and discomfort.

It is out of this custom of women sharing with other women "outside the camp" that some historians are now concluding that the broader identity of the Hebrew nation was forged. Prior to this time, tribes tended to remain separated. Men fought and worked together, but generally according to tribe. It was the practice of women being integrated across family lines that led to a genuine national identity.

Many of the customs related to home and family arose from this practice, too. The Law of Moses does not define how a wedding is to take place, how a funeral is to be conducted, what should happen ritually to celebrate the Sabbath, the details about a family's celebration of a child being affirmed as an adult, and so forth. These customs very likely arose as women shared ideas with one another, just as customs today work themselves into our culture when one person or group innovates a new practice. Others see it, find it meaningful, and copy it. This goes on and on until a new practice has been adopted throughout the culture.

Finally, it is important to note that these women took a break from their normal routine, albeit a required one. Given the extended nature of families at that time, the women who were clean took over the chores of those who were unclean. The woman who was unclean was given a time to regain her energy and renew her strength, as well as to renew her ability to conceive and bear children.

Israelite women were pregnant a great deal of their adult lives. Families were large. Very few women had the luxury of a week off each month. Still, most women probably had at least five or six week-long retreats from work and responsibilities each year.

What does this have to do with modern-day women?

Today women's lives tend to revolve around work. Effort and time are our measures for how we spend our lives, or how we "spill" our lives out to others. When we do not take time and energy for activities that are conducive to spiritual life, we breach our relationship with our Creator.

When that happens, we are wise to "get out of the camp" for a while, get our priorities back in line, rest our bodies, and rejuvenate our spirits, and then return to our activities and responsibilities with a fresh perspective, a renewed commitment to the Lord, and an eagerness to see a procreation and regeneration of spiritual life in ourselves and others.

A woman certainly can get out of her routine and spend time by herself. But there's wisdom in joining with other women, for a mutual sharing of ideas and comfort. A woman has the capacity to understand another woman in a way no man can.

It is out of women sharing their best and most godly experiences in the use of power that women better learn how to apply power to everyday life. They learn how to become more skilled, efficient, and effective at seducing, subduing, transacting, training, influencing, witnessing, praying, and persevering.

One of the things we have seen happen in the last thirty years is that a fairly small group of women seem to have defined how, when, and over whom a woman should exercise power.

There's a great need for Christian women to come together across family lines (in our case, denominational lines) to share their insights into what it means to be a Christian in today's world. As women do this, creativity virtually explodes. Women challenge one another to excellence. They train one another in practical skills. They make decisions that impact their families and ultimately, their communities, states, and nation. And they find commonality in Christ Jesus and what He has done and continues to do in each of their lives.

Taking a break personally with the Lord and collectively before the Lord is the foundation for a woman growing in her ability to apply her power.

·························
Courage Is Being Willing to Give All

To have courage means to be willing to stand even if nobody else will. It means being willing to give your all, even to the giving of your life.

Rahab is one of the most courageous women in all the Bible. When two Israelite spies came to her home in Jericho, she gave them shelter. And when the king of Jericho sent word to Rahab to turn over her guests, she hid the men among the stalks of flax on her roof and she said to the king's messenger, "Yes, those men came here, but I didn't know where they were from. Just as it was getting dark and the city gate was about to be shut, they went out of the city. I don't know where they were going but perhaps if you hurry, you can catch them." (See Josh. 2:4–5.)

After the king's men left to search for the spies, Rahab came up to the two men on the roof, and as they sat together in the darkness she said, "I know that the LORD has given you the land" (Josh. 2:9). She explained to them how word had reached Jericho about the parting of the Red Sea, and about the defeat of two great Amorite kings west of the Jordan River. She said, "As soon as we heard these things, our hearts melted; neither did there remain any more courage in anyone because of you, for the LORD your God, He is God in heaven above and on earth beneath" (v. 11).

What a phenomenal declaration of faith! Rahab believed in the God of the Israelites even before she met an Israelite.

Rahab then did what no one else in Jericho had dared to do. She said, "I beg you, swear to me by the LORD, since I have shown you kindness, that you also will show kindness to my father's house, and give me a true token, and spare my father, my mother, my brothers, my sisters, and all that they have, and deliver our lives from death" (vv. 12–13). The men agreed.

Rahab then helped them get out of Jericho by hanging a rope from a window of her house, which happened to be built on the wall. She told them to head for the mountains and hide there three days.

What a bold and courageous woman! She stood up to the king of her city. She was bold enough to negotiate a deal with two men she didn't know. She helped two men escape into the night. And she did all this with a knowledge that if either her lie, her deal, or her help in the escape ever came to light, she surely would be killed.

Perhaps the most courageous period of Rahab's life, however, was not while she was speaking to the king's messenger, hiding the Israelites, negotiating with them, or helping them to escape. It came during the days that immediately followed.

For three days the men hid in the mountains as Rahab had suggested. And then they made their way back across the Jordan to Joshua and the rest of the children of Israel. Three more days passed before Joshua sent word through the camp, "Prepare to move out." Still more days passed while the people crossed over the river and while the men healed after being circumcised. And then the marching around Jericho began.

For six days Rahab and her family probably watched in wonder, expectation, and fear as the children of Israel marched once each day around their city. And then on the seventh day, they probably felt a mix of fear and excitement as the Israelites marched seven times around Jericho.

All the while, a scarlet cord hung from the window in Rahab's home, the agreed-upon sign that her household was to be spared when all the rest of Jericho was destroyed.

Rahab had to have the courage not only to speak when necessary, but also to remain silent when necessary. She had to be willing to give up her life in Jericho and move with her family to a completely new environment with new customs, religion, and practices. She went from being a city girl in a well-established city, to being a nomadic wanderer in search of conquest.

Rahab's life was spared, and she married an Israelite by the name of Salmon. Their son was Boaz, the man who redeemed Ruth. Her distant descendant was Joseph, husband of Mary and Jesus' earthly father.

Rahab's courage to save two Jewish spies centuries later impacted the life of the Savior who gives us the courage to spy out evil enemy territory and claim it for the kingdom of God.

....
Taking Action Is Applying Power

Once we have taken a break, realigned our priorities, and renewed our relationship with the Lord, we can take courage! The Lord has a task for us today. And who knows how far-reaching the implications of our application of power may turn out to be!

We grow in power and then we *go* in power.

We don't need to go very far in any given day to find a need, hear a request, face an enemy, or encounter a situation that calls for a righteous application of our God-given power as women.

The need or situation will compel us to respond. It is as we respond that we apply power.

In many cases, we won't have time to consider, *Which type*

of power should I employ? Rather, we will tend to react instinctively. That's because this power resides in each of us. We don't have to conjure it up or dig very deep to find it.

At other times, we will be faced with a situation and have ample time to weigh our options and make concerted, conscious choices.

In either instance, we must keep in mind that our exercise of power must be open. As Christian women, we are admonished by God's Word not to operate in secret. The Lord Himself, and only the Lord, has the privilege of dealing with us in the secret places of our heart. In our relationships one to another, we are to be candid and without guile.

An elderly woman once came to me after I had given a presentation about godly uses of power. She said with a mischievous grin, "I think I'm going to go home and throw around some of my power." She paused for a moment, the twinkle still in her eye, and then added, "As soon as my husband wakes up."

She said more than she knew. We need not announce our every move or give a play-by-play description regarding our behavior and motives as if we were sportscasters or fashion-show runway commentators. But we do need to make certain that those to whom we apply or direct our power are "awake."

We have no authority to use an unfair advantage. Our use of power must be without any taint of brainwashing. We must allow others to make full use of their free will.

We also need to recognize that we do not have unlimited power of any kind, nor will we ever. Unlimited power is an attribute of our eternal and infinite God. Nor do we have privilege to apply unbridled power. Raw, uncontrolled power is nearly always manifested as rage or brutality. Neither are godly. Unfair, unlimited, and unchecked power are all forms of power gone amuck.

The net result of our application of power must always be to build up others, and in the process, to build up ourselves. We do not seduce people to bring them down, or attempt to influence people so that we can gain an upper hand, or deal in transactions that cause loss to another person. The godly use of power is to build up people, even as we tear down in prayer the spiritual strongholds that are keeping them from growing into their full stature in Christ Jesus. The Scriptures call this process *edifica-tion*, the building up of people to the fullness of Christ's nature.

Toward that end, we are always to take actions that propel a person toward Christ. We nudge, not push. We encourage others to open their eyes, we don't pry their eyes open. We pull others up, not push them down. We lead by example, rather than using a whip from behind.

....

Will Women Ever Have Too Much Power?

A woman asked me if I thought a woman could ever have too much power.

No. We can't have too much power, either individually or collectively as women. But we can have too little of Jesus.

The needs in our world are massive. Need and pain are present in every person we encounter. Put any two people together and you find mutuality of pain, and also a potential for those two people to cause each other further pain. Take a look at any population sample and you'll find needs and hurts unique to that particular group.

We can never have too much power because needs will always present themselves to challenge and totally exhaust all the power we have!

We can come unplugged from the Source of our power. We all know that feeling. We must guard ourselves against it every day. The Lord doesn't leave us. But we tend to wander away, like sheep. (See Isa. 53:6.) He doesn't stop inviting us to His wedding celebration. But we forget to keep our lamps filled with oil. (See Jesus' parable of the ten virgins in Matt. 25:1–13.)

God's path doesn't swerve. We stray from it in hot pursuit

of temptations. (See Isa. 30:9–11.) He doesn't change. But we seem to change from moment to moment, blown about, it seems, like leaves in the wind or sand in the desert. (See Heb. 13:8.)

To grow strong and mighty in power, and then to apply that power in full force, we must stay connected to, closely related to, intimately associated with the Source of our power, the Holy Spirit of Almighty God, the same Holy Spirit that indwelled Christ Jesus.

We must know God, follow Him, serve Him, obey Him, and give Him our all to the best of our ability. The Lord taught us to conclude all of our petitions to the heavenly Father by yielding to Him the kingdom, the power, and the glory. His power is ultimate. We are mere vessels to convey it to our world.

Several times I have stood in awe at Third World women who were engaged in extremely demanding physical labor. One mental picture is especially vivid to me. A group of us were in northern China a number of years ago when we saw a very small, older woman pulling a large cart filled with coal up a slope. The very fact that this woman, who must have been at least sixty years old, could move such a heavy cart even an inch was amazing to me. I watched her for several moments, observing closely how she kept her shoulders forward at all times, and how she took small even steps. Finally, I said to our guide, "She's incredible. How does she do it?" He replied very matter-of-factly, "She doesn't stop to think about how. She does it because there's a bowl of rice waiting for her and each member of her family at the end of the day."

As Christian women, we have large, heavy carts and upward slopes awaiting us. Let's keep our eyes and motion forward. Let's take small, evenly paced steps if need be. Let's not get bogged down in the hows. Instead, let's keep our eyes on the goal: that we and each member of our family and circle of friends might one day sit down together at the great wedding feast of the Lamb, that marvelous and eternal celebration awaiting us with the Lord in heaven.

His is the kingdom. And on that glorious day, we will turn over every parcel and facet of earth that we have claimed for Him so that He might rule and reign over it forever.

His is the power. He is the Source of all our ability, capacity, and inspiration.

And His is the glory. All of our applications of power must serve to crown Him the King of kings, and Lord of lords.

Women have what it takes! And we can take from the enemy what is rightfully ours and rightfully His, if we will take a break, take courage, and then take action in His name and for His sake.

About the
Author

Jan Dargatz, Ph.D., has been a teacher, magazine editor, university vice president, and founder/CEO of a company. She is the successful author of many books, including *Simple Truths*, *52 Simple Ways to Build Your Child's Self-Esteem*, and *10,000 Things to Praise God For* and is a frequent speaker on spiritual growth at women's Bible conferences and retreats. Dargatz currently lives in Tulsa, Oklahoma.